# Simple Soldered Jewelry & Accessories

## A Crafter's Guide to Fashioning Necklaces, Earrings, Bracelets & More

# Simple Soldered Jewelry & Accessories

## A Crafter's Guide to Fashioning
## Necklaces, Earrings, Bracelets & More

Lisa Bluhm

A LARK/CHAPELLE BOOK

A Division of Sterling Publishing Co., Inc.
New York / London

**EDITOR**
James Knight

**ART DIRECTOR**
Stacey Budge

**COVER DESIGNER**
Chris Bryant

**ASSISTANT EDITOR**
Julie Hale

**ASSOCIATE ART DIRECTORS**
Lance Wille
Shannon Yokeley

**ART PRODUCTION ASSISTANT**
Jeff Hamilton

**EDITORIAL ASSISTANCE**
Delores Gosnell

**ILLUSTRATOR**
Orrin Lundgren

**PHOTOGRAPHER**
Stewart O'Shields

A Lark/Chapelle Book

Chapelle, Ltd., Inc.
P.O. Box 9255, Ogden, UT 84409
(801) 621-2777 • (801) 621-2788 Fax
e-mail: chapelle@chapelleltd.com
Web site: www.chapelleltd.com

Library of Congress Cataloging-in-Publication Data

Bluhm, Lisa, 1969-
 Simple soldered jewelry & accessories : a crafter's guide to fashioning necklaces, earrings, bracelets & more / Lisa Bluhm. --
    p. cm.
 Includes index.
 ISBN 1-60059-030-6 (hardcover)
 1. Jewelry making.  I. Title.
 TT212.B58 2007
 745.594'2--dc22

                                2006027892

10 9 8 7 6 5

Published by Lark Books, A Division of
Sterling Publishing Co., Inc.
387 Park Avenue South, New York, N.Y. 10016

Text © 2007, Lisa J. Bluhm
Photography © 2007, Lark Books, A Division of Sterling Publishing Co., Inc.
Illustrations © 2007, Lark Books, A Division of Sterling Publishing Co., Inc.

Distributed in Canada by Sterling Publishing,
c/o Canadian Manda Group, 165 Dufferin Street
Toronto, Ontario, Canada M6K 3H6

Distributed in the United Kingdom by GMC Distribution Services,
Castle Place, 166 High Street, Lewes, East Sussex, England BN7 1XU

Distributed in Australia by Capricorn Link (Australia) Pty Ltd.,
P.O. Box 704, Windsor, NSW 2756 Australia

If you have questions or comments about this book, please contact:
Lark Books
67 Broadway
Asheville, NC 28801
(828) 253-0467

Manufactured in China

ISBN 13: 978-1-60059-030-6

For information about custom editions, special sales, premium and corporate purchases, please contact Sterling Special Sales Department at 800-805-5489 or specialsales@sterlingpub.com.

For information about desk and examination copies available to college and university professors, requests must be submitted to academic@larkbooks.com. Our complete policy can be found at www.larkbooks.com.

# Contents

# Introduction

SIMPLE SOLDERED JEWELRY & ACCESSORIES is an easy-to-follow guide that introduces you to the joy of making soldered jewelry and decorative items for the home. The primary technique you'll use is simply a matter of melting a quick-setting metal alloy onto copper foil that's wrapped around pieces of glass. If you can use a glue gun, you can use a soldering iron. Trust me—it's a technique that's easy to learn, and with practice and a little patience, you'll master it in no time.

The first two chapters show you the tools you'll need to get started and introduce you to the simple techniques you'll use to create the projects in this book. As you work, refer back to these chapters for basic how-to pointers or to answer any questions you may have about the tools you're using. I recommend practicing the various techniques a few times to get a feel for both the material and for the process of putting soldered glass pieces together. Once you're comfortable with the fundamentals, move on to the fun part: making the projects!

I hope you'll see the instructions for the projects in a couple of different ways: You can use them to re-create the pieces as they're shown, or you can use them as a conceptual springboard, launching your creativity into new directions. My personal favorites are the ones that are the most unique and allow for a lot personalization—pieces like the Sassy Daisy Wrist Cuff on page 114, Scrapbook Frames on page 118, and Picture Perfect Pixie Collages on page 136, are just a few that let an artist cut loose and get creative.

Why did I write this book? I love to share this craft with people. Making soldered art and jewelry has brought me a lot of joy and satisfaction over the years. I began teaching classes across the country and found teaching to be extremely satisfying. Helping people find a new creative outlet and seeing the light go on in their eyes as they discover a new hobby is a huge rush for me. This book is a natural extension of organizing and teaching classes.

I remember when I started working with soldered art, it did seem a little intimidating at first. I made many mistakes and learned a lot from them. I wrote this book to give you the benefit of my experience. In other words, I made the mistakes so you won't have to. Whether you're a beginner or an old hand at the craft, I hope you'll find this book helpful in achieving success and realizing the joy of tackling new challenges. Dive in, experiment, and let your creativity be your guide.

# Chapter 1

# Essential Tools and Materials

IF YOU'RE NOT FAMILIAR with soldered art and jewelry making, be prepared for something new and exciting. When you see the projects featured in this book, you may be surprised to learn that you don't have to be a metallurgist or master jeweler to pull off stunning designs early on in your new hobby. In fact, the concept is simple, and the techniques are pretty easy to learn.

Creating the centerpiece for each project is essentially a three-step process. You'll start by sandwiching handmade designs of paper or textiles between two pieces of cut glass (whether or not you'll cut the glass is up to you). Next, you'll learn how to wrap the edges of the piece with copper foil. Why? Solder won't stick to glass but it will stick to the metallic surface of the copper foil tape. In the last step, you'll melt and "pour" the solder onto the foil, where it will cool quickly and set in place. This creates the solid metal frame around the piece. Think of the process as making small, art-filled capsules of glass.

This chapter covers the basic tools and materials needed to get started right away. However, before you start, spend a few moments considering your work space.

## Setting Up Your Work Space

Having a proper work area is a foundation for success. The space should be neat and tidy. Well, OK…maybe that's a dream for some of us, but it does need to be safe, at the very least.

Always work in an open area with adequate ventilation. Most standard-sized rooms will do nicely. If necessary, solder near a window so you can take advantage of the extra light and also be able to open it for added circulation. Some people choose to work on their kitchen table, while others opt for creating a studio for themselves.

Since you'll be using a hot appliance (the soldering iron), your primary work surface needs to be fire-retardant. For me, the best thing to use is a big piece of glass. The one I use came from an old picture frame. Of course, the glass is fireproof, and when solder drips onto it I can re-melt and reuse it. Glass cutting boards also make a great work surface. There are even fire-retardant mats available.

## Tool Setup

It's important to arrange your work area so that you can put your tools back in the same place each time you use them. Doing so makes it easy to find what you need when you need it, and it'll also help you avoid accidents, such as reaching and grabbing a hot iron by the wrong end.

Place the iron and iron holder on the same side as the hand you'll use to hold it while soldering. Make sure the cord is not draped across your work area. If the cord is going to hang off the edge of a table, tape it down at the edge so the cord's weight doesn't pull the hot iron off the table.

### GLASS CUTTING AREA

If you choose to cut your own glass, you'll need a special area that provides a hard, smooth, flat surface. Any object on the surface can cause the glass to crack while applying cutting pressure. After cutting glass, clean the area with a damp towel to get rid of any little glass pieces. Do not use your hand to scoop away glass shards or dust.

# Project Tools and Materials

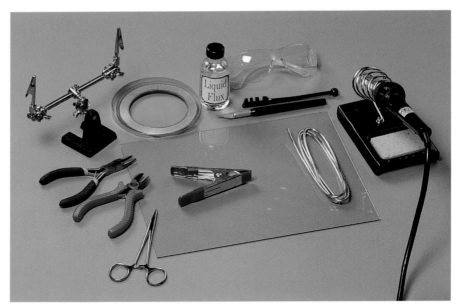

Using the right set of tools is essential for success in almost any project. This is particularly true for today's solder artist. I've tested and tried many different tools, and the ones I use the most are in the mid-to-low price range. Just because a tool costs more doesn't mean it will do a better job. In this section, I've listed many of the tools you'll need, what they're used for, how they work, and what you should look for when choosing new ones.

## Soldering Tools

Here's a list of basic tools you should have for your soldered art workspace. Most—if not all—of these can be found in craft stores or home improvement stores at very reasonable prices.

### SOLDERING IRON

The soldering iron is an electric, high-temperature heater that's used to melt the solder. It should be lightweight, have a replaceable tip, and should get hot enough to melt the solder. I like to use irons that are no lower than 25 watts.

Always place the iron in an iron holder. Turn the iron on when you are ready to solder, and turn it back off when you are done. Don't turn the iron on and let it sit idle for long periods of time. It takes only a few minutes to warm up. Once you have your project foiled and ready to go, plug in the iron.

When first heating up, a new iron may smoke and you may smell something that smells like plastic burning. This will stop after the first few uses.

## SOLDERING IRON TIP

Tips aren't interchangeable between brands of irons. You should use only the tips that are made specifically for certain models. I have tested many styles of tips as well. The type of tip that works best for me is a flat chisel or screwdriver tip ranging in size from $1/8$ to $1/4$ inch (the measurement refers to the width across the very end of the tip). My favorite size is $5/16$ inch.

Most tips are made of copper with a plating over the copper. For my money, the best type of tip has an ironclad plating (this process increases the life of the tip). Poorly plated tips deteriorate quickly, sometimes after just a few uses.

Taking care of the tip is extremely important to successful soldering. Keeping the tip clean and tinned is the key (tinned means to have a coating of tin on it). To clean the tip, use a wet synthetic sponge to wipe the tip during use. Remember, wipe the tip against the sponge, don't press the tip down into it. Pressing the tip into the sponge can cause the sponge to melt onto the tip. Make sure to keep the sponge wet during your work session.

Some tips come with a coating of paint on the tip to protect against oxidation. When the iron heats up, the paint will turn black and crackle off.

You'll need to "tin" the tip even if it comes pre-tinned. To do this, just melt some solder onto the tip and wipe it off on the wet sponge. The tip should appear shiny. This is how you want to keep the tip looking so that it doesn't lose its *wetting capability* (this means its ability to melt the solder). When a tip gets black with oxidation, it becomes unwettable; although it gets hot, it won't melt the solder.

Make it a habit to wipe off the tip every time you turn the project and rest the iron in the iron stand.

If the iron tip does become unwettable, you can do several things to make it useful again:

- Melt solder onto the tip and wipe it off repeatedly until it looks shinier.

- Use a lead-free tip tinning compound that is made out of a flux paste embedded with solder particles (simply put your hot iron tip into it and it will re-tin the tip).

- As a last resort, you can use a file, a brass bristle brush, or a sanding stone to remove the black coating (just be sure you don't remove the plating).

- If none of these work, then it's time to replace the tip.

## IRON STAND

You'll need a place to set the hot iron while you're not soldering. Laying it on the table is not a good idea for obvious reasons. (Yes, I've absentmindedly set my iron down on the table, and the smell of burning wood has reminded me why that's a bad idea.) To avoid this, I highly recommend using an iron stand. The stand should have a heavy base to prevent it from tipping over, a steel safety coil for resting the hot iron, and a place for the wet sponge.

Make sure the coil is screwed on tightly to the base. The coil will get hot when the iron is in it, so avoid touching it while you're working. Clean and rinse the sponge after each use.

## Holding Clamp

You'll need something to hold your project as you work. Because of the type of projects you'll be making, it's necessary to hold the pieces upright. A metal clamp with a rubber handle is ideal for this need. The rubber on the handle will protect you when the metal on the clamp gets hot. The clamp will act as a stand for the piece you are working on. Match the size of the clamp to the size of the project you are working on. Alligator clips work well for smaller projects and for clamping on items to be soldered to the project.

My favorite is the jeweler's extra hands tool. It consists of movable arms with alligator clamps on the ends. It can easily hold projects and allow you to move them around without continuously unclamping them.

## Pliers

For most projects, a pair of needle-nose pliers with a rubber grip will do the job. The pliers are needed to hold objects, mainly jump rings, in place while you solder them on.

Another option is a locking hemostat. Though they're traditionally used in the medical field, they're also quite useful for holding onto small items while soldering.

## Grozing Pliers

These specialized pliers are used to nip away at the glass, straighten up a not-so-straight cut, or remove unwanted pieces of glass. They have serrated tips with one curved side and one flat side. The flat side is used for grabbing the glass and snapping off larger sections. The curved side is used for nibbling away small pieces of glass.

## Glass Cutter

Don't let the name fool you. The glass cutter doesn't actually cut the glass; it scores it so that it will break cleanly when pressure is applied. The blade wheel is usually made of steel or carbide and ordinarily isn't sharp enough to cut a person. In addition, glass cut-ters usually have a ball at the end. This is used to tap the glass after it's scored. Gentle tapping causes the score to run and break.

Some glass cutters come with a self-oiling chamber that allows cutting oil to be fed to the tip area. However, if your glass cutter doesn't have an oil chamber, simply soak a rag with oil and run the blade across it. It takes only a small amount. You can use glass cutting oil, sewing machine oil, even cooking oil.

## Files

Files can be used on the solder and the glass. All kinds of files can be used, from fingernail files to jeweler's files. Files can smooth out rough glass edges or bumpy solder.

# Tools for Beading

Many of the projects in this book call for beads to be either threaded on strands or used as decorative embellishments. Here are a few tools that can make adding beads to your pieces much easier.

## WIRE CUTTERS

It's good to have a couple of different kinds of wire cutters: a lightweight one to be used for smaller wires, and a heavier wire cutter for thick wires and metals. Make sure you're using the right cutter for the job; it's very easy to ruin the blades of a cutter on something that's too heavy.

## CONCAVE BENDING PLIERS

This is my favorite of all my beading tools. One jaw is round, with a 1.5 mm tip that graduates up in size. The other jaw has a channel down the middle that fits the first rounded jaw; the jaws actually fit around each other. It's used to make rounded shapes and loops easily (this is what I use for all my bead dangles).

## FLAT NEEDLE-NOSE PLIERS

These come with serrated or smooth surface jaws. The serrated jaw gets a better grip on things but can leave marks on the metal. The serrated pliers are great for opening and closing jump rings. Smooth-jawed pliers are good for bending wires or holding onto wires without leaving marks.

*Examples of specialty beading tools and pliers: a.) Crimp pliers b.) Needle-nose pliers c.) Concave bending pliers d.) Round-nose pliers e.) Wire cutters f.) Flat needle-nose pliers*

## ROUND-NOSE PLIERS

Both jaws on the round-nose pliers are round and taper to a narrow point. Use these to make loops or rounded curves on the wires. They come in different tip thicknesses as well.

## CRIMP PLIERS

Use crimp pliers to close crimp tubes or beads. You can also use them on bead wires to finish off the end of the wires with a loop.

The crimp tube is strung onto the wire, and the wire is strung back down through the tube to make a loop. The tube is placed in the back chamber of the pliers and squeezed, crimping the middle of the tube. The crimped bead is moved to the front chamber of the pliers and squeezed again to fold the tube in half and give it a finished look.

# Finishing Tools

There are many options for finishing soldered art and jewelry. Perhaps you'd like a smooth finished look for jewelry pieces, or a rustic look for more artistic pieces. Whatever your preference, here are some finishing techniques to try as you go through this book.

## HAND FILES

These simple little tools come in all shapes and sizes, and can work wonders on rough spots or bumpy soldered edges. They can also file down sharp or crooked edges of glass. For heavy-duty sanding jobs, start with a heavy grit, move to a lighter grit, and end with a buffer.

## ROTARY TOOL

Rotary tools with different types of bits can be very useful. Sanding bits can be used to smooth glass or solder. Engraving bits can be used to etch glass. Any basic rotary tool will work. They're easy to find and relatively inexpensive.

## SANDING DRUM

Sanding drums have little sanding bands that fit over them and come in different grits. For bigger jobs, start with a heavier grit and work up to a lighter grit. If you want a brushed appearance to the metal, do not use the lighter grits.

*Hand files*

## FINISHING STONE

My personal favorite! Finishing stones are impregnated with fine emery abrasive. They're ideal for cleaning and polishing solder and creating a smoother surface.

## DIAMOND OR ENGRAVING BIT

A diamond or engraving bit can be used to grind on the solder, but it also can be used on the glass.

## SOFT CLOTHS

For cleanup and polishing, soft cloths work best. Just cut up an old T-shirt (make sure it's a clean one) and use the pieces for washing the projects or buffing off wax. Then throw them away when they've served their purpose.

*Rotary tool*

# Soldering Materials

As you begin working and making your own glass and soldered objects, you'll find alternatives that work to your liking better than others. In the meantime, here's a list of basic materials to get you started.

### LEAD-FREE SOLDER

Since you'll be making jewelry and other items for the home—things that you'll handle and touch regularly—you'll want to make sure you use lead-free solder.

You need to know what is in the solder you're using and how to use it safely. If the package doesn't provide this information, you can usually find it online from the manufacturer or contact the company for a MSDS (material safety data sheet).

A good standard to look for is lead-free solder that contains tin, copper, and a small amount of silver. If you want a shinier finish, use a solder with more silver in it. The best I have found has four to six percent silver in it. Just bear in mind, the higher the amount of silver, the higher the solder's melting point will be.

Solder most often comes as a solid wire or a rosin core wire. The solid wire is pure solder. A rosin core wire has flux in the center of it and can be rather messy and smelly to use. I prefer to use the solid wire type.

*Lead-free solder*

### FLUX

Flux is used to clean and deoxidize the surface. Its application creates a barrier between the metal and the air. If you don't flux, the solder won't stick.

Most flux contains hazardous acid. I prefer to use a water-based, non-acidic liquid flux that is much more user friendly.

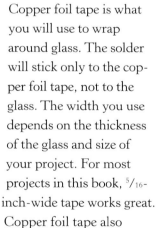

### COPPER FOIL TAPE

Copper foil tape is what you will use to wrap around glass. The solder will stick only to the copper foil tape, not to the glass. The width you use depends on the thickness of the glass and size of your project. For most projects in this book, $5/16$-inch-wide tape works great.

Copper foil tape also varies in thickness. The thinner the mil, the easier it can tear or curl while applying it. The thicker the mil, the more difficult it can be to fold, burnish, and wrap around curves. I've found that thicknesses ranging between 1.5 mil to 1.0 mil are good for the projects in this book.

*Various types of copper foil tape*

Some projects call for tape that has a different backing, usually black or silver. You'll want to use these when the back of the tape can be seen through the glass and a copper color peeking through the piece just wouldn't look good. Decorative-edged tape provides a wavy border on one edge and a straight edge on the other.

### GLASS

Most of the glass used for the projects in this book is a clear 1 mm thick glass. This is the same thickness of glass used for microscope slides. While you want the glass to be thin to keep the finished pieces light, glass any thinner than 1 mm breaks too easily.

Glass can be bought in precut shapes and sizes at most craft stores. Stained glass also is available in many different colors and textures. Glass from picture frames can also be used.

Dollar stores are a great source for inexpensive frames that use glass. Sometimes the glass has a bluish hue to it and can range in thicknesses.

### WIRE

Wire can be used for decorative touches or decorative hangers. The wire needs to be made of copper, brass, or nickel. Aluminum or coated wires can't be used—the solder won't stick. Most silver-looking wires are copper wire that has been plated with nickel or tin. When a coated wire is heated up, the plated finish will often burn away, revealing the copper wire. Using a solid nickel wire that looks silver all the way through will prevent this from occurring. Wire comes in several gauges. The higher the gauge number, the thinner the wire. A 20-gauge wire is good for hanging attachments, while a 26-gauge wire is good for decorative embellishments.

### JEWELRY FINDINGS

Findings are the various components jewelers use to assemble their pieces. Jewelry findings come in all shapes, sizes, and styles. They can be made from various metals: base metal, nickel, copper, brass, sterling silver, gold, and pewter. Pewter shouldn't be used in these projects because it has a melting point close to that of solder.

### DECORATIVE METAL EMBELLISHMENTS

Metal embellishments can be found in many places: toggle clasps, decorative box corners, shaped wire clips, picture hangers, scrapbook embellishments, decorative brads, decorative studs, washers, hardware, etc. I'm always on the lookout for interesting metal items I can use on my projects.

# Bead Materials

If you're not familiar with beading or have never visited a bead store, you may feel overwhelmed (or overly excited) by all the goodies they have to offer. No doubt you'll quickly pick up on what suits your style best, but until then, here's a cheat sheet to use as a starting reference.

## BEADS

Beads come in thousands of styles, shapes, sizes, materials, and price ranges. It doesn't matter what type of beads you use as embellishments or foundational pieces. If you'll be soldering directly to the beads, they need to be made of glass, stones, crystal, or any type of material that can withstand the heat.

## BEAD WIRE

Bead wire is made of several smaller stainless steel wires stranded together and coated with a nylon coating. The wire is very strong, but flexible. The more strands that are used, the more flexible the wire is, so a 19-strand wire will be more flexible than a 7-strand wire. The wire also is available in several colors.

## CRIMP TUBES

Crimp tubes or crimp beads are used to finish off the ends of the bead wires and secure the loops at the ends for clasp attachments. Tubes are easier to crimp with crimping pliers.

## HEAD PINS

These are used throughout the projects in this book to make bead dangles. A head pin is a wire with a small head on the end. Most commonly, head pins will have a ball end.

## EYE PINS

Eye pins are wires with one loop on the end. Beads are strung on and then a loop is made at the other end. Eye pins can be used as connectors.

## CHAIN

Chain is sold by the foot from most bead stores. Chain also comes in many kinds of metals, styles, and sizes.

## LEATHER

Leather is an affordable and casual choice for jewelry. It comes in cording, lace, and flat pieces. It also comes in a variety of colors and styles.

## COIL ENDS

Coil ends are used on the ends of the leather or other cords to finish the ends and add an attachment for the clasp to hold onto.

## JUMP RINGS

Jump rings are generally used for attaching items to jewelry. It's good to have several sizes on hand to use for different purposes. I prefer nickel jump rings because they keep their silver color after being heated.

## ART MATERIALS

As you're planning and designing your projects, keep in mind the bulk of the items you choose to place between the panes of glass. Bulky objects can easily be turned into a paper image by using a copier or a scanner. Many of the pieces you'll be making are small and require only a small amount of material.

When choosing art for adding flair and "life" to your work, your options are practically limitless:

• Paper

• Pictures

• Fabric

• Ribbons and trims

• Ephemera ("doodads" that might otherwise be thrown away)

• Embellished or discarded glass

## OTHER "ARTFUL" THINGS

The world is full of interesting objects just waiting to be discovered—and sandwiched between glass for soldered art—so keep your eyes peeled. For bulky or large items, just remember you can scan them or copy them to make them into a paper image. Try dried flowers and leaves, silk flowers and leaves, artwork, children's craft projects, buttons, clothing items, decorative knickknacks, books, pottery, picture frames, beads, fibers, stickers, and many more. You're limited only by your imagination.

18

# A Few Words about Safety

Since you'll be working with hot tools, chemicals, and glass, you need to consider a few basic safety issues. Use common sense in working with these tools and materials. Always follow the manufacturer's guidelines and recommendations for everything you use.

## Safety Glasses

Always wear safety glasses. Solder sometimes pops and spits. When this happens, little droplets are sent airborne and they can end up in your eyes. Flux can spit and pop, too, and sometimes emit irritating vapors. You'll also be cutting glass, sanding projects, etching glass, and many other potentially harmful activities, so protect your eyes.

## Dust Mask

A dust mask can keep you from breathing in dust and fine debris generated while sanding. If you're concerned about vapors, masks are available with fume traps.

## Gloves

Wear gloves when you're working with patinas. They're strong chemicals and should never touch your skin. Again, follow the manufacturer's suggested precautions.

## Children

Soldering is not recommended for children. Keep all your tools, chemicals, and materials out of children's reach. Try not to work on solder projects while children are present. A child could easily touch a hot iron or glass scraps.

*Chapter 2*

# Creating Soldered Glass Pieces

This is where the fun begins. After getting your work area set up and ready, you'll want to dive right in and start making soldered glass objects. In this chapter, you'll learn the basic techniques of building your designs, placing them between pieces of glass, wrapping the edges of your piece with copper foil tape, and applying the solder to the edges.

You'll probably want to practice these techniques a few times before applying them to projects or altering valuable keepsakes. That way, you'll get familiar enough with them to create pieces with smooth, confident lines and decorative embellishments.

In addition, this chapter covers techniques for adding jump rings and decorative embellishments to soldered pieces, as well as basic jewelry-making tips. Refer to this chapter often as you go through the projects later in the book.

## Cutting Glass

I remember a movie in which a spy had to break into an office. The only thing standing in his way was a large glass door. I was amazed to see him pull out a glass cutter and easily cut a large circle out of the glass so he could reach in to unlock the door.

Well, that's not how glass cutters work—they merely score the glass so it breaks evenly. With a handheld glass cutter, you can cut glass to the size and shape you want. If cutting glass is new to you, try using a scrap piece of glass to practice on first.

Photo 1. Marking the cut line

Photo 2. Scoring the glass with a glass cutter

## Scoring the Glass

Learning how to score glass in a straight, precise line is the best way to start. Remember, work on a hard, smooth surface and wear protective eyewear.

1 Trace or draw your line onto the glass with a permanent marker. The permanent marker will not show once the piece is wrapped with copper foil tape (see photo 1).

2 Hold the glass cutter in your fingers like a pen, perpendicular to the glass, straight up and down. Place it on the top inside edge of the glass.

3 Push the glass cutter away from you firmly (see photo 2). You might hear or feel a little scraping on the glass; that's OK. When you get to the other edge, try not to roll the glass cutter over the edge, but stop just at or before the edge. You will see or feel a small line. This is the score line where your glass will fracture and break apart.

## Breaking the Glass

Surprisingly enough, there's more than one way to break a piece of glass. Here are some ideas on how to ensure precision as you work.

The first option you can try is placing the glass over the straight edge of a table with the score line on top and lined up with the table's edge (see photo 3). Press down on the glass hanging over the edge of the table.

The glass will break apart along the score line (see photo 4).

Another option is to use the ball end of the glass cutter to tap against the back of the glass, causing the scored line to run. Keep tapping along the glass until the entire scored line has fractured apart. This method works well for long cuts or curvy cuts.

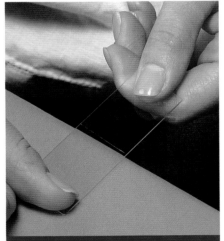

Photo 3. Using a table top to break the glass

Photo 4. Breaking the glass

Also try using grozing pliers. Align the jaws on one side of the score line, with the flat side of the jaw on top of the glass; grasp the other side of the glass with your hand (see photo 5). Squeeze lightly on the handle, just enough to hold onto the glass, while prying the glass apart in a downward and outward motion (see photo 6).

Photo 5. *Grozing pliers can be used to break glass.*

Photo 6. *Separating the scored glass*

# Evening Up Not-So-Even Cuts

Try a variety of methods to make your glass edges come out nice and even.

### USING GROZING PLIERS
If a cut has jagged edges or needs to be straightened up a bit, use the grozing pliers as a glass muncher. Nip away at the glass by grasping small sections of glass and squeezing the handles closed while prying away in a downward and outward motion (see photo 7).

### SMOOTH IT BY SANDING
If only small amounts of glass need to be evened up, use a heavy metal file or a sanding bit in a rotary tool to smooth out the rough or uneven edges.

### MASTERING CURVED CUTS
Curved cuts require more cutting than just the shape itself. There is no way that the spy I told you about earlier could have simply popped out a circle of glass.

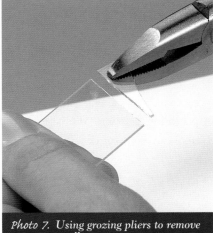

Photo 7. *Using grozing pliers to remove small remnants*

In order to remove a circle of glass, break lines need to be made out to the edges of the glass.

1 Trace and score the curved shape. Tap the glass, causing the score to fracture.

2 Score several break lines around the shape. Start at the edge of the scored shape, working out to the edges of the glass. When all the break lines are scored, tap the back side of the glass to cause them to fracture.

3 Use grozing pliers to remove the glass pieces from the shape one at a time, until the shape is free.

If you're cutting pieces of glass for front and back sides and they do not quite match up, it won't be noticeable once the pieces are wrapped with the foil tape and soldered. Crooked edges of glass can be evened out by manipulating the solder to be thicker or thinner along the edges. If the shape you have cut is too difficult to duplicate, you can use an alternative backing. Aluminum foil tape or foil scraps make a nice silver backing and are easy to cut.

23

# Assembling the Piece

After you have created a composition of paper, textiles, or photographs that you like, you'll want to sandwich them between the cut and shaped pieces of glass (see photo 8).

Be sure to be as accurate as possible as you cut your artwork. You don't want any edges of paper, string, ribbon, or other material sticking out from between the glass. Carefully line up the glass and art.

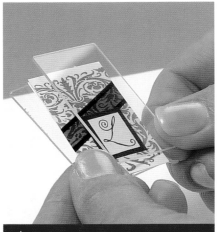

*Photo 8. Placing the paper design between the glass panes*

# Copper Foiling Technique

Once you have your glass cut, sanded, and the piece assembled, you're ready to apply copper foil around the edges. Copper foil is used because it is easy to form and bend, solders well, and is inexpensive. Remember, solder will stick to the foil (not the glass) where it will set quickly, giving you a metal framework around your glassed-in art.

The copper foiling technique is sometimes referred to as the "Tiffany method" because the technique was used to create the famous Tiffany lamps. While a lot has changed since the days when those lamps were manufactured, many of the principles remain the same. The solder itself is the "glue" that holds the piece together.

## Preparing the Glass

Smooth out any rough edges of glass so they don't poke through the copper foil. Clean any residue or oils off the glass. Make sure items pressed between the glass don't extend past the glass edges.

## Applying the Foil

The object of applying the copper foil tape is to center the glass on the foil tape so you have equal amounts of overlap on the front and back sides.

1 Use your thumb and index finger to peel and press the sticky side of the foil tape to the edges of the glass, while looking down on the glass to make sure it is centered (see photo 9). Rotate the glass in your other hand, working your way around the edges while peeling back the paper backing as you go.

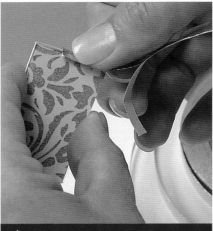

*Photo 9. Wrapping copper foil tape around the edges of the glass*

24

**2** Continue wrapping around the glass until you are back at the starting point. Overlap the end of the foil tape over the starting point about ¹/₄ inch (see photo 10). Cut or tear off the excess tape.

**3a** *Straight-Edged Projects.* Once the tape has been applied to the edges, it needs to be crimped over the front and back sides. Start in the middle between two corners and, using your thumb and index finger, fold and push the foil flat against the glass (see photo 11). Work your way out to the corners; neatly and carefully tuck the side foil edges under the top unfolded edge of the foil tape. This will create a mitered corner once the rest of the tape is crimped, like wrapping a present (see photo 12). Fold over the other edges and smooth flat to the glass.

**3b** *Round-Edged Projects.* For rounded projects, crimp the foil in evenly around the edges a little at a time. Continue working your way around the project, crimping a little more each time. There will be many little creases in the tape (think of a foil pie tin as an example) (see photo14).

**4** The foil now needs to be burnished, which means to press and seal the foil tape to the glass. You can use the ball end of the glass cutter, a clothespin half, a bone folder, your thumbnail, or anything with a smooth, flat surface (see photos 13 and 15).

Photo 10. Overlapping the tape by ¹/₄ inch

Photo 11. Folding over the edges of the tape

Photo 12. Pressing down the tape edges

Photo 13. Burnishing the foil

Photo 14. Using a thumbnail to crease the tape

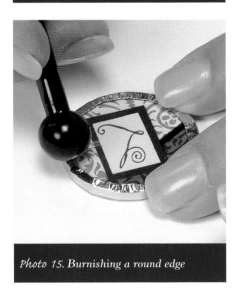
Photo 15. Burnishing a round edge

By burnishing, you're making sure the foil is firmly stuck to the front and back sides of the glass, smoothing out air bubbles, wrinkles, creases, or corner folds in the foil tape. Make sure not to rub too hard—this may cause the foil tape to stretch and tear. If that happens, it's best to remove the entire piece of foil tape and re-foil the whole thing. If you try to create a patch with another piece of foil tape it will lift while you are soldering. If you try to "fill in" a torn spot with hot solder, the solder will not stick to the glass, only to the foil tape, and a void will be visible.

5 The last step is to trim the foil tape if needed. Use a craft knife and cut through the foil right onto the glass (the glass will not get scratched) (see photo 16). Peel away the excess foil tape. Some adhesive residue may remain and can be cleaned off later while finishing the project.

Photo 16. Use a craft knife to trim the excess foil

# Soldering Techniques

When soldering for the first time, you may feel like a fish out of water. To take the pressure off yourself, consider it practice. Wrap a piece of glass and solder and re-solder it until you feel more comfortable with the task. You'll begin to feel how much pressure to apply, how much solder to add, and how to hold the tools in your hands.

## Positioning the Project

Place the clamp onto the edge of the project (never clamp it in the middle; the pressure will break the glass). Choose a clamp size that will hold the project firmly but without damaging it.

## Applying Flux

Paint a thin coating of flux onto the edge of the copper foil tape (see photo 17). It is best to flux just the edges you're working on first instead of all the edges at once, because the flux can evaporate as you're working on the project. The key is a thin coating; too much flux can cause spitting and popping while soldering. You also don't want the flux to get under the tape and seep under the glass. Once you've fluxed the copper foil tape, you need to solder it. Fluxed copper foil tape that's left unsoldered will patina and become difficult to solder onto. If the solder isn't flowing, or if the flux has evaporated, simply reapply the flux.

Photo 17. Brushing on flux

## Hand Positioning

If you're right-handed, hold your soldering iron in your right hand and the solder coil in your left hand. The iron should be held in a pencil grip, close to the tip end of the iron. The iron should be held at a 45° angle to the edge of the project, with the flat sides of the tip of the iron horizontal to the edge.

# Tinning Technique

For beginners I recommend using a tinning technique first. Tinning is when a thin coat of solder is "painted" onto a surface or object. Some solder artists always begin a project by tinning it first, and then going back and adding a bead of solder (this means an edge of solder that has a smooth, thick, rounded edge).

1 Place the tip onto the left end of the project edge. Touch the tip lightly onto the edge of the copper foil.

2 Press the solder onto the top flat side of the tip. The solder should start to melt and flow down the tip (see photo 18).

3 Once a small amount of solder is on the foil edge, pull the solder coil away from the tip so that you are not adding more solder to the edge (see photo 19).

4 Use the iron tip in a painting motion, lightly touching the tip to the foil and causing the solder to melt (see photo 20).

5 Spread the solder over all edges of the foil, adding more solder as needed for a thin coat.

6 Be careful not to press too hard with the iron or hold the iron in one place too long; you may burn through the copper foil tape. Once you remove the iron from the solder, it will set quickly. Continue to tin the

*Photo 18. Starting the solder*

*Photo 19. Flowing the solder onto the edge*

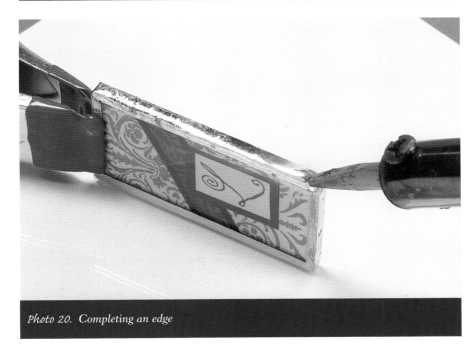

*Photo 20. Completing an edge*

rest of the copper foil tape by rotating the project in the clamp and covering all the edges. The glass will get hot too; use caution when turning the project.

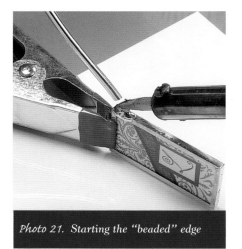

## "Beaded" Technique

In soldering jargon, a *beaded edge* of solder running along an edge of a piece means it has a plump, rounded appearance. Creating this kind of line takes practice, but isn't necessary to enjoy what you're doing. As long as your edges are thick enough for structural strength, you can use various finishing techniques to smooth out and round them later.

1 To create a thick, beaded edge, start by placing the tip onto the left end of the project's top center edge. Touch the tip lightly onto the edge of the copper foil; press the solder onto the top flat side of the tip. The solder should start to melt and flow down the tip, coating the top edge of the solder and flowing down the front and back sides.

Once the solder has reached the foil tape, slightly lift the tip off the foil, letting it hover just above the tape. You want to have a "bridge" of liquid solder flowing from the tip to the copper foil tape (see photo 21).

2 Move your hands together in one smooth motion across the edge from left to right. The harder you press the solder onto the tip, the more solder you'll have melting and flowing onto the edge of the project. It's much easier to work with a smaller amount of solder on the edge than more. Solder can always be added later to make it thicker.

If too much solder is creating lumps on the edges, you can re-melt the thicker lumps of solder and spread it along the edges to even it out. If there is still too much solder, hold the project at an angle above your glass work surface and re-melt the solder. The excess will drip off your project onto the glass.

3 When you get to the end of an edge, bring the soldering iron tip straight off the edge at a downward angle, separating the tip from the solder. Check the front and back sides of the copper foil to make sure they have been covered with the solder. If more coverage is needed, you can add more solder; or if there is enough solder on the edge, it can be re-melted, allowing it to flow over the exposed copper foil. To help the solder flow over the front and back edges, place the iron tip on the front (or back) edge, centering the flat surface of the iron tip onto the outermost edge of the project. Working from left to right (again in a smooth, steady motion), melt the solder, allowing it to flow over the front (or back) areas of exposed copper foil tape.

4 Once the solder is set on the first edge, unclamp the project and turn it so a new unsoldered edge is on top. The glass will remain hot, so use caution when handling it. Use pliers if necessary to handle the glass.

5 Continue to turn and solder the project until all the copper foil tape is covered. Once it is covered, go back and smooth out any lumpy spots if needed, or add more solder. When smoothing or adding solder, apply flux first so the solder will flow smoothly. For some projects, you may want a rustic, lumpy look to the edge, while on others you may want a smooth beaded edge.

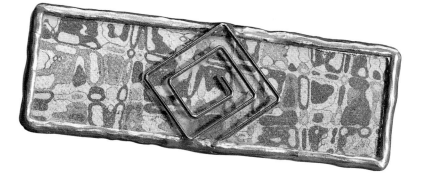

# Adding a Jump Ring

To add a jump ring to the project, you will need to melt the solder while simultaneously pressing the jump ring into it. There are several different methods for doing this. While some may seem easier than others, all can be mastered easily with practice. Most important is that you have enough solder for the jump ring to "sink" into so the solder will flow through and over the jump ring.

## PLIERS METHOD

1 If more solder is needed for attaching the jump ring, you will first need to add a mound of solder to the edge. To do this, place the hot tip near the edge and press the solder into the tip, just until the solder starts to flow.

Lift the tip and solder off the edge, leaving a mound of solder (see photos 22 and 23). If there is a point on the mound, use the iron to flatten it.

2 Place a jump ring with the opening side down in a pair of pliers or locking hemostat. Paint flux onto the jump ring on the opening side where it will be soldered (see photo 24).

3 Using the pliers in one hand, place the fluxed part of the jump ring onto the hard mound of solder. Bring the edge of the tip in from the front side and touch the point of the tip to the mound of solder (see photo 25). Once the solder mound begins to melt, push the jump ring down into it

Photo 22. Adding a "mound" of solder

Photo 23. Pulling up to create the mound

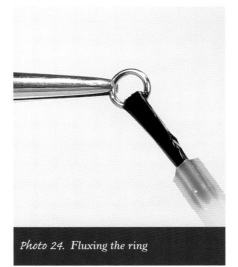

Photo 24. Fluxing the ring

Photo 25. Heating the mound of solder

Photo 26. Pushing the jump ring down into the heated solder

while removing the iron from the mound (see photo 26). Hold the jump ring still until the solder has set.

If the jump ring is not in the correct position, grasp the jump ring with the pliers, re-melt the solder, and move the jump ring. The same also can be done if a jump ring needs to be removed. Always hold the jump ring in place to keep it from moving while melting the soldered edge that is around it. However, if you melt and re-melt too many times in one spot, you risk burning through the copper foil tape.

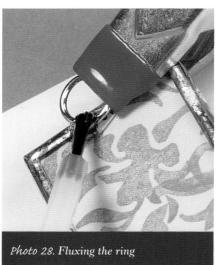

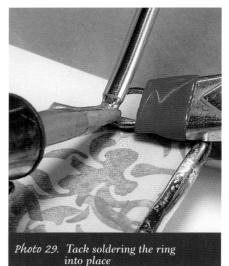

Photo 27. Clamping the ring

Photo 28. Fluxing the ring

Photo 29. Tack soldering the ring
into place

## CLAMP METHOD

If holding your hands steady is not an option or proves to be frustrating, try clamping the jump ring to hold it in place.

1 Place the jump ring onto the project's back edge. Use a small clamp to hold the jump ring in place (see photo 27).

2 Paint flux on the jump ring (after it is clamped) where the solder will be flowing onto it (see photo 28). Melt the solder on the edge so that it flows onto the jump ring and "tacks" it in place (see photo 29). If there is not enough solder on the edge, melt more solder onto it.

## JIG METHOD

A jig is a device used to maintain the correct positional relationship between a piece of work and the tool during assembly. This method can take more time setting up than actually attaching the jump ring, but if accuracy is your primary goal, it's worth it.

The jeweler's helping hands tool can be used as a jig by setting it up so that it holds the jump ring in place on the project while you add the solder.

1 Place the project in a holding clamp with the edge to be soldered at the top. Place a jump ring into a clamp on the jeweler's helping hands tool.

2 Flux the jump ring where it will be soldered onto. Position the jeweler's helping hands tool so that the clamped jump ring is resting on the soldered edge of the project.

3 Melt a small amount of solder onto the jump ring and the soldered edge of the piece (see photo 30).

Photo 30. Using a jeweler's helper as a jig

## ALTERNATIVE JIG METHODS

Other types of premade jigs are also available for purchase, or you can fashion one yourself from materials you already have around the house. The idea is to lay the project flat, wedge it in place so it won't move, and use something half the thickness of the project to lay the jump ring onto so you can solder it in place. Here's an easy method to think about:

1. Lay the project onto your glass work surface. Surround the project with glass pieces one layer thick (the same thickness of glass as used in the project).

2. Tape the surrounding glass pieces down so they won't move.

3. Lay a fluxed jump ring onto the glass, positioning it so that it's touching the soldered edge of the project (see photo 31). If needed, tape the jump ring to the glass (not the project) with a small piece of tape to keep it from moving (see photo 32).

4. Melt a small amount of solder onto the jump ring and the soldered edge of the piece (see photo 33).

*Photo 31. Using glass as a jig*

*Photo 32. Securing the ring with tape*

*Photo 33. Tack soldering the ring into place*

Photo 34. Clamping the wire

Photo 35. Fluxing the wire

Photo 36. Tack soldering the wire into place

## Adding Decorative Wire

To create a free-form wire design, try this:

1 Lay a length of wire onto the project edge. Clamp the end of the wire in place (see photo 34).

2 Flux the wire where it will be soldered together (see photo 35).

3 Use your iron tip to melt the solder on the edge, allowing it to flow onto the wire and "tack solder" it in place (see photo 36). Make sure not to melt too much solder; you could cover the wire and lose its decorative details.

4 Bend and form the wire in a shape to complement the project. Beads or other embellishments can be strung onto the wire as well.

5 Tack solder the wire to the soldered edge as needed to hold it in place and maintain its shape. Use a clamp as needed when tack soldering the wire.

## Adding Decorative Metal Embellishments

Many different types of metal embellishments can be soldered onto projects to add to the design, function, and texture. Metal gets hotter and retains heat longer than glass, so use caution and common sense when handling it.

Many decorative metals are made from brass and then plated with silver plating. This plating will burn off when heated, exposing the metal underneath. To make it silver again, use the tinning method.

- Coat the metal with a thin layer of flux (see photo 37).

- Melt a small amount of solder onto the iron tip.

- Use the tip to "paint" over the metal surface spreading a thin layer of solder to cover the exposed metal (see photo 38). Do not use too much solder or the decorative elements will be covered.

Photo 37. Fluxing the front of the metal piece

Photo 38. Coating the metal with solder

Photo 39. *Filling in the concave piece with solder*

For items that are concave on the back side:

- Paint flux on the back concave side.

- Melt solder onto the back, filling in the concave areas (see photo 39).

- Clamp the item onto the soldered project.

- Use the iron to melt the solder added to the concave side onto the soldered edge of the project.

# Finishing Techniques

When you finish the soldering part of a project, you'll need to clean off any flux or other residues from all the surfaces. If flux remains on the solder, it'll cause oxidation and discoloration. Oxidation can't be stopped completely, only slowed down. One trick is to slow down the process by using a finishing wax.

Once the project is clean, you can apply several different finishing techniques to give the solder a different look—from a polished shine to a rustic finish. For the beginning solder artist, finishing techniques can help improve the appearance of a not-so-great soldered edge. Experiment on scrap material to see how different techniques look.

## Cleaning Pieces

On most of the projects, there will be a slight bit of cleaning up to do from the actual "construction" process. Here are some basic tips on how to safely clean glass and soldered objects.

### REMOVING WATER-SOLUBLE FLUX

If you are using a wate- soluble flux, water will remove any flux residue left on the project. The residue is not always visible but it's there. If the project has paper or other material between the glass, you'll not want to submerge the project under water.

Water can seep under the tape and get between the glass, which could ruin the project.

For projects with paper between the glass, use a damp rag to wipe off the project until all the residue is removed, then dry everything thoroughly. For projects without paper, rinse under running water.

### REMOVING OTHER FLUX

Some fluxes may require a special flux remover solution. Follow manufacturer's instructions for using the flux remover.

### REMOVING ADHESIVE OR BLACK SPOTS

During the soldering process, the adhesive on the copper foil tape may ooze from the tape and leave a residue on the glass, or black spots on the solder. To remove the adhesive, use a craft knife to scrape the adhesive off of the glass or the solder.

## Sanding the Solder

Once you're done soldering the projects, use your fingers to feel around the soldered edges for any sharp or rough spots. The spots can be smoothed out using various sanding techniques. Sometimes it's easier to sand off an area instead of trying to re-melt the solder to fix it.

## HAND SANDING

One of the easiest ways to sand the edges is to use fingernail files. They can be found in various grits from heavy to fine. Choose the grit necessary for the amount of filing needed to be done. Start with the heaviest grit needed and work up to a finer grit to smooth-out the sanded surface. A buffing file works well as the last step in giving the soldered edge a nice shine. You may also use sandpaper, metal files, diamond files, steel wool, or any other type of sanding material you may have on hand (see photo 40). Make sure it is small enough so that you will not be scratching the glass while sanding the soldered edge.

## ROTARY TOOL SANDING

A rotary tool is fun to use and can make the sanding process easier and faster (see photo 41). Choose bits according to how much sanding is needed. Generally all you need is a heavy sanding drum and a finishing stone. The heavy sanding drum will remove the solder fast; you can actually remove too much and expose the copper foil tape underneath. The finishing stone works well for smoothing out sanded edges and minor bumps, and gives a nice smooth, shiny appearance to the solder. Once you have mastered soldering, all you need is the finishing stone to polish up the soldered edges.

## MAKING A TEXTURED SURFACE

Skip the buffing or finishing stone step if you want to give the soldered edge a textured appearance. You can leave it with the brushed look or use a diamond tip in a rotary tool to give it an interesting textured edge.

Photo 42. Applying finishing wax

# Using Finishing Wax

There are finishing waxes specifically formulated for use on soldered projects. Generally this wax is made from carnauba wax and micro particles of abrasive material. You also can use any kind of carnauba wax, such as the type used on your car. The wax is applied to the soldered edges (and even the glass) by using a brush or a rag. Let the wax dry to a hazy white finish. Once the wax is dry, buff it off with a soft cloth.

There are now metal polishes on the market that give a dramatically higher shine to solder. Look for the type that can be easily applied, wiped off, then buffed to a high shine.

Photo 40. Using a hand file

Photo 41. A rotary tool makes sanding easier.

# Applying Patinas

A patina is a finish that changes the color of metal upon application. Patina solutions are available at most craft stores. In order for the patinas to work properly, you must start with a thoroughly clean, dry, and unwaxed surface. It's important not to track other chemicals into the patina, which could prevent it from working properly. Always pour patina into a nonmetal container. Dispose of any unused patina properly; don't add it back into the original container. Patina can be applied with a brush, cotton ball, cotton tip swab, or a rag. Gloves must be worn, since patinas contain acid and are corrosive.

## BLACK PATINA

Black patina has a higher acid content than copper patina. Take care not to leave it on the glass too long because it can etch or stain it. Dip an applicator of your choice into the patina and wipe over the soldered edges. It'll start to darken pretty quickly. Once the metal has darkened, use a wet rag to wipe off the patina from the surface (or rinse under water for projects without paper under the glass). Dry and reapply the patina to make the finish darker. Once the finish is dark enough and has been washed and dried thoroughly, it can be coated with a finishing wax.

## COPPER PATINA

The copper patina is a little more troublesome than the black. Apply it to all the soldered edges; keep applying it to increase the depth of the copper color. Once you are finished applying the copper patina, do not rinse with water; instead, wipe it off with a dry rag.

# Applying Color to Soldered Pieces

For variety, try one of these methods to give your pieces extra interest.

## USING PAINT

Before painting soldered edges, make sure the surface is clean and give it some "tooth" by sanding the edge lightly. This will help the paint to adhere to the metal. Check the label to see if it works on metal surfaces. Most paints for metal surfaces will stay on pretty well without flaking off. Acrylic paints will flake off easily and are best left for decorative pieces.

## APPLYING INK

Because of the popularity of rubber-stamping, there's a wide array of inks available. Many are specifically for nonporous surfaces, such as metal and glass. Try using them on your projects for interesting effects.

## ALCOHOL-BASED INK

Alcohol inks are available in pen, pad, or liquid form. They are not necessarily made for use on metal but they do work. They give a translucent coating of color. Apply the ink to the soldered edges with a pen, a brush, or other applicator. It dries quickly so you'll need to work fast. To keep the color from coming off, seal it with a clear brush-on lacquer.

## PERMANENT INK

Like alcohol inks, permanent ink is available in pen, pad, or liquid form. The ink is applied to the glass or solder with pens, brushes, sponges (my favorite), or any other applicator of your choice. The permanent inks can come off but stay on better than the alcohol type inks.

# Beading Basics: Techniques for Working with Wire

Figure 1

Figure 2

Figure 3

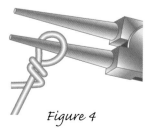

Figure 4

If you're an accomplished jewelry maker, you already know the joy and creativity involved with putting together your designs. For those who are just starting, take heart: the process of learning is fun, and it's pretty simple once you master the basics.

Here are a few techniques to practice before diving into the jewelry-making projects later in this book. Refer to these steps later and review them as needed.

## How to Make Simple Loops

Start with 6 inches of wire and work with a pair of round-nose pliers. Make a sharp 90° bend about $^1/_2$ inch from one end of the wire, as shown in figure 1. This measurement will vary, depending on how large a loop you want to make; with practice, you'll get to know how much wire to allow for it.

Hold the wire so that the longer portion points to the floor and the short, bent end is pointing at you. Grasp the short end with the round-nose pliers, holding the pliers so that the back of your hand faces you. The closer to the tips you work, the smaller the loops you can make. Keeping the tips themselves stationary, rotate the pliers up and away from you (see figure 2). Be careful not to pull out the right-angle bend you made earlier. Stop rotating when you've made half the loop.

Slide the pliers' tips back along the wire a bit and resume the rotation. To prevent the loop from becoming misshapen, make sure to keep one of the pliers' tips snug inside the loop as you make it, so that the loop is being formed by a combination of rotation and shaping around the "mandrel" of the pliers. Keep working, sliding the pliers back as needed, until the loop is closed against the 90° bend (see figure 3).

A *bead loop* is made by enclosing a bead between two loops. Another option is to start with an eye pin, so that you'll have to fashion only one closing loop. This method is used a lot in this book.

Of course, there are hundreds of variations of these basic links. Loops and links can be attached to each other with jump rings or linked directly together as you make them.

A *wrapped bead loop* is a simple variation of the bead loop. Use an extra length of wire for the 90° bend. Once you've made the loop, reposition the pliers so that the lower jaw is inside it. Use your other hand to wrap the wire's tail around the base of the loop several times, as shown in figure 4. Slide on one or more beads and, if the design calls for it, repeat the loop-forming process at the other end to make a wrapped bead loop (see figure 5 ). Trim off any excess wire.

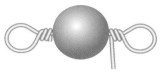

Figure 5

## Opening and Closing Loops

Just as with jump rings, use a pair of pliers to open and close loops. Twist the cut end sideways while keeping the other side of the loop stationary. As with jump rings, pulling it open any other way will distort the loop's shape. Be sure to tighten any gaps in loops after you've attached your links.

Figure 6

## Twisting

Only square wire can be twisted. Round wire won't show the twisting properly.

To create twisted wire in no time at all, work with a pair of pin vises. Insert each end of a piece of wire into a pin vise, tighten the chucks, and twist them in opposite directions until you like the look you've achieved. If you have only one pin vise, secure the other end of the wire in a clamp or table vise (or in a pair of pliers if you have just a short quantity to twist). You can also use this tool to twist two lengths of the same wire together, creating a heavier look, or to twist together two different colors of wire.

Figure 7

## Making Spirals

To create flat spirals, use the tip of a pair of round-nose pliers to curve one end of the wire into a half-circle or hook shape about $^1/_8$ inch in diameter (see figure 6). Use the very tips of the pliers to curve the end of the wire tightly into itself, aiming to keep the shape round rather than oval, as shown in figure 7. Hold the spiral in flat-nose pliers and push the loose end of the wire against the already-coiled form (see figure 8); as you continue, reposition the wire in the pliers as needed.

Figure 8

# Chapter 3

# Beautiful Basic Pieces

*This chapter is designed to get you comfortable with the feel of working with solder and glass. All the projects in this chapter use simple microscope slides. They're the same shape and size time after time. Since the projects involve no glass cutting, there's nothing to distract you from quickly learning the basic soldering techniques.*

# Letter Pendant

*Here's an easy way to start: make a basic pendant using standard microscope slides and your choice of decorative elements.*

## MATERIALS

Strip of jacquard ribbon, 1 x
   3 inches
2 glass slides, 1 x 3 inches
Decorative clip art back-
   ground
Clip art letter
Copper foil tape
Lead-free solder
Large jump ring
Ball-chain necklace

### INSTRUCTIONS

1 Cut the ribbon to fit between the glass slides.

2 Cut out a large letter or image (look in magazines, or print out enlarged letters or clip art from a computer).

3 Sandwich the ribbon and cut out art between the glass slides.

4 Wrap the edges with the copper foil tape.

5 Solder all the edges.

6 Solder the large jump ring to the top of the pendant.

7 String the ball-chain necklace through the jump ring.

# Cheery Holiday Ornaments

Topped with festive bows or ribbon loops, these decorations make perfect gifts. Silver stickers and other embellishments add extra sparkle for the season.

# Vintage Angel Ornament

MATERIALS

Vintage holiday clip art
Glue
Glitter
2 pieces of decorative paper for
  background, 1 x 3 inches
2 glass slides, 1 x 3 inches
1 silver decorative sticker
1 strip decorative silver trim
Copper foil tape
Lead-free solder
1 large jump ring
Ribbon

**INSTRUCTIONS**

1 Cut out vintage-looking art from a card or other source.

**FRONT**

2 Choose something in the picture you'd like highlighted with glitter. Apply the glue to that part of the art. Sprinkle the glitter onto the glue. Let it dry.

3 Glue the cut out art to the strip of decorative paper. Add the silver flourish sticker toward the top of the composition.

**BACK**

4 Using the same process from step 3, create a different composition for the back.

5 Place both strips together and sandwich them between the glass slides.

6 Wrap the piece with the copper foil tape.

7 Solder all the edges.

8 Solder a large jump ring onto the top edge of the ornament.

9 Thread the ribbon through the jump ring to hang the ornament.

# Easy Retro Ornaments

### INSTRUCTIONS

**MATERIALS**

Holiday clip art images
2 strips of colorful paper for
   the background, 1 x 3 inches
4 glass slides, 1 x 3 inches
Copper foil tape
Lead-free solder
2 decorative hangers
Glue
Ribbon

1 Round up old holiday cards or clip art with retro images or themes. Make collage using the decorative paper and your holiday clip art. Trim it to fit between the slides.

2 Place the collage between the glass slides. Make sure you like the composition on both sides of the piece.

3 Wrap the edges with the copper foil tape.

4 Solder all the edges.

5 Solder a decorative hanger along the top edge of each.

6 Thread the large ribbon through the hanger to hang the ornament.

# New Life for Found Objects

*On this brooch, a simple square paper clip becomes the center of attention. The piece shows the flexibility of soldered art—with a little imagination, almost any object can be reborn.*

**INSTRUCTIONS**

1 Trim the paper to fit between the glass slides. Cut two separate pieces: one for the front, and one for the back.

2 Place both pieces between the two slides. Make sure the paper doesn't extend past the edges of the glass.

3 Wrap the edges with the copper foil tape.

4 Solder all the edges.

5 Lay the square paper clip on the front of the piece. Clamp it in place.

6 Paint flux onto the edge of the paper clip where the solder will be melted to it. Be careful not to apply too much flux; a thin coat will do.

7 Using the edge of your soldering iron tip, melt the solder that is already on the edge so that it just barely flows onto the edge of the clip, "tacking" it into place (see page 30). Do this on the top and bottom edges where the paper clip touches the soldered frame.

8 Mark the backside where the pin will be attached. Test the location to be sure the pin will open and close properly.

9 Add a small bump of solder where the pin will go (see page 29).

10 Paint flux onto the back side of the pin.

11 While holding the pin attachment, melt the bump of solder and push the pin into it. Hold the pin steady until the solder is set.

**MATERIALS**

Decorative paper
2 glass slides, 1 x 3 inches
Copper foil tape
Lead-free solder
Square paper clip
Set of bar pin findings

# Snazzy Storage Labels

*Use your newfound soldering skills to create customized labels for your home's organizational needs. Tie these decorative nameplates to baskets, containers, file boxes, or anything else where scribbled-on masking tape just wouldn't do.*

## MATERIALS

Clip art letters, words, or labels
2 glass slides, 1 x 3 inches
Copper foil tape
Lead-free solder
2 large oval jump rings
Ribbon

## INSTRUCTIONS

1 You can generate graphic labels from a computer, or clip out appropriate words and phrases from magazines. Any printed material will do. Using a copier allows you to enlarge or reduce the size to fit. Trim the clip art to fit between the slides.

2 Sandwich the label between the two pieces of glass.

3 Wrap the edges with the copper foil tape.

4 Solder all the edges.

5 Solder a large oval jump ring to each side.

6 Thread the ribbon through the jump rings.

# Chapter 4

# Get the Angle on Using Glass Squares and Rectangles

*In this chapter, the focus shifts to working with various smaller shapes of cut glass. If you choose to cut glass for your projects, there are handy templates in the back of the book (see page 143) to help you draw accurate cut lines for common straight-edged shapes. Just remember the old saying "practice makes perfect." A little practice goes a long way in glass cutting. You'll see impressive results in no time.*

*This chapter also introduces some basic beading projects. Be sure to look back to page 36 for tips on making head pin loops and other helpful advice.*

# Dichroic Glass Bracelet

*The surprisingly colorful display from dichroic glass gives this bracelet high-impact appeal.*

## INSTRUCTIONS

1 Cut four panels of each color of dichroic glass. Make each 1 inch high and ½ to ¾ inch wide. Don't worry about making the cuts perfectly straight. Shapes that end up slightly different will add character to the finished piece.

2 Wrap the pieces with the copper foil.

3 Solder all the pieces.

4 Solder two small jump rings on both sides of each panel about ⅛ inch in from the corners. Use a permanent marker to mark the spot where you'll solder the jump rings.

5 Use the medium jump rings to connect the panels. Be sure to alternate the colors. Thread a silver bead onto the medium jump ring first, then thread it through the small jump rings on the glass panels. Make sure the bead is on the front side of the bracelet. Close the jump ring to secure.

6 Attach the magnetic clasps to each end.

### MATERIALS

2 coordinated colors of
   dichroic glass scraps
Copper foil tape
Lead-free solder
32 small jump rings
18 medium jump rings
18 round silver beads, 2 mm
2 magnetic clasps

# Blue Topaz Necklace and Earrings

Nature's beauty is reflected in this striking combination of silver and sparkling topaz. Add decorative paper that complements this combination, and you'll make a strong statement about your natural creative instincts.

## MATERIALS

Decorative paper

2 pieces of glass, 1 inch square

4 pieces of glass, ¾ inch square

Copper foil tape

Lead-free solder

Silver wire

5 head pins

Blue topaz chip beads

16 silver spacer beads

8 bicone crystal beads, 4 mm

19-strand bead wire (at least
18 inches long)

2 crimp tubes

2 jump rings

Lobster clasp set

Pair of purchased ear wires

## INSTRUCTIONS

1 Cut your choice of paper to fit between the glass pieces.
Fit the glass and paper together.

2 Wrap the pieces with the copper foil tape.

3 Solder the edges of all the pieces.

4 Using round-nose pliers, bend the silver wire into a small circle.
Continue bending the wire around to create a spiral (see page 37). Make two large spirals for the necklace and four small spirals for the earrings.

5 Solder the spirals to the top and bottom edges of each piece.

6 String four head pins with the blue topaz chips. Create a loop at the end of each (see page 36).

7 String one head pin with two blue topaz chips, a silver spacer bead, a bicone crystal bead, a silver spacer bead, and two more blue topaz chips. Make a loop at the end.

8 Attach two head pins to the bottom spiral of the necklace's charm, keeping the bicone bead head pin in the center.

9 Cut a length of bead wire 18 inches long for the necklace. Slip the wire through the top spiral on the necklace charm. Center the charm so

52

the ends of the bead wire come together. String a silver spacer bead, a bicone bead, and another silver spacer bead onto both wires. Slide the beads down the wires until they're secure at the top of the spiral.

10 String 10 topaz chips onto each side of the bead wires.

11 String a silver spacer bead, a bicone bead, and a silver spacer bead onto one side. Continue this pattern two more times up the wire. Copy this pattern on the other side.

12 After the third set of silver spacer beads and bicone beads, fill the rest of the wire with the topaz chips.

13 At each end, secure the wire with a crimp bead with a small loop at each end.

14 Attach the lobster clasp set and close the jump rings.

15 For the earrings, attach a dangle (made with topaz chips) to the bottom of each spiral. Add the ear wires to the top spiral.

# This Charm Bracelet Makes a Statement

*The idea behind this charm bracelet is simple: to celebrate the creative spirit. It only makes sense, then, that there's plenty of room left for you to add your own charms and other personal touches.*

### INSTRUCTIONS

1 Cut enough of the paper and letters to make all the charms you need. Remember, each of the charms will have two sides. Place the paper pieces between the pieces of glass. Wrap each charm with the copper foil tape.

2 Solder all the edges of each charm.

3 Attach jump rings to the top of each charm.

4 Attach the soldered charms to the chain, spacing them evenly. Count the number of links between each charm for proper spacing.

5 Thread eight head pins with a single diamond-shaped bead. Make a loop at the top of each pin (see page 36).

6 Thread nine head pins with one square bead, one silver spacer, and one square bead each. Make a loop at the top of each.

7 Attach other charms of your choosing to the links between the soldered charms, spacing them as evenly as possible.

8 Fill in the remaining spaces with the bead dangles.

9 Make sure all your jump rings are closed. For added security, you can solder the jump rings closed once the charms are attached.

10 Attach the toggle clasp set at the ends.

MATERIALS

Festive paper
Alphabet clip art
12 pieces of rectangular glass, 1 x ¾ inches
Copper foil tape
Lead-free solder
30 jump rings
Length of silver-link chain that best fits your wrist
8 diamond-shaped beads
17 head pins
18 square beads
9 silver spacer beads
10 pewter charms
Toggle clasp set

# Wire Monogram Choker

*This simple project calls for a hand-formed wire letter to adorn the top of the pendant.*

## INSTRUCTIONS

1 Trim your choice of paper to fit inside the glass. Place the paper between the glass pieces.

2 Wrap the glass with the copper foil tape.

3 Solder all the edges.

4 Form a wire letter using the wire alphabet template found on page 142.

5 Lay the wire letter onto the front of the soldered charm. Adjust the wire as needed to connect with the soldered edges. Use a clamp to hold the wire letter onto the surface. Flux the contact points of the wire letter. Melt solder onto the wire to "tack" it in place (see page 30).

6 Flux the silver bead and solder it onto the top edge of the charm.

7 Measure the velvet ribbon to fit around your neck and add 4 inches to one end.

8 Thread one end of the ribbon through the shank on the button. Tie a knot to secure. Trim the excess ribbon. Glue the end flat to the underside of the ribbon.

9 Adjust the fit and mark the ribbon where the loop will need to be. Tie a loop at the other end of the ribbon. Try the loop over the button to make sure it fits, then tighten the knot. Elasticized ribbon makes it easier to get a smaller loop, since the loop can stretch to fit over the button. Trim the excess ribbon.

## MATERIALS

Decorative paper
2 pieces of glass, 1 x ¾ inch
Copper foil tape
Lead-free solder
20-gauge wire
Large-hole silver bead
16 to 18 inches of elasticized velvet ribbon
Silver button (shank style)
Glue

# Two Classic Necklaces in Silver and Gold

In these two necklaces, gold chain and gold accessories are contrasted with the natural silver tone of solder. The combination is a great way to heighten the dramatic appeal of your jewelry.

## MATERIALS

2 rectangular pieces of glass,
    1½ x ½ inch
Decorative paper
Copper foil tape
Lead-free solder
6 gold jump rings
Red jasper briolette, 8 mm x
    12 mm
4 inches of 22-gauge gold-tone
    wire
33½ inches of gold-tone, small-
    link chain
8 flat silver saucer beads, 3 mm
8 silver ball head pins
4 red jasper round beads, 3 mm
4 silver beads, 2 mm
3 gold-tone teardrop beads
3 inches of matching gold-tone
    link chain
Gold-tone lobster clasp set
Gold bead dangle

## Double-Chain Necklace (shown on left)

INSTRUCTIONS

1 Cut the paper to fit between the glass pieces. Place the paper between the pieces of glass. Apply the copper foil tape. Solder all the edges.

2 Solder one gold jump ring onto the top and bottom of the pendant.

3 Thread the wire through the briolette. Make a simple twist, and then make a loop at the other end (see page 36). Thread the loop through the bottom jump ring on the pendant and close the wire in place.

4 Cut an 18-inch piece of gold-tone chain. Attach the pendant to the center of the chain with a jump ring.

5 Cut another piece of chain 15½ inches long.

6 Thread one silver saucer bead onto a silver ball end head pin. Add a round red jasper bead, another silver saucer, and top those with a 2 mm silver bead. Make a loop at the top and trim the wire. Make a set of four of these bead dangles.

7 Measure 4 inches from the end of the shorter chain and attach one bead dangle. Measure over 1 inch and use a jump ring to attach a gold teardrop bead to the chain. Continue the pattern until you attach the fourth bead dangle. It should be 4 inches from the other end of the short chain.

8 Join the two chains together at both ends with a gold jump ring. Attach the lobster clasp set onto the jump rings.

9 Attach three inches of the matching gold link chain (as an adjuster chain) on the end opposite of the lobster clasp. Finish the end of the adjuster chain with one gold bead dangle.

# Multi-Beaded Necklace

1 Cut the paper to fit between the glass pieces. Place the paper between the glass. Apply the copper foil tape. Solder all the edges.

2 Solder one gold jump ring to the top and another to the bottom of the pendant.

3 Thread the wire through the briolette and then twist it a couple of times. Leave an open loop at the top of the briolette wire. Thread the open end through the bottom jump ring on the pendant. Close the wire.

4 String one gold bead onto the gold-tone eye pin and make a loop on the other end. Connect it to the top jump ring. Attach the other end through a link at the center of the chain.

5 Thread the silver, gold, and red jasper beads onto head pins (one per pin), finishing each with a loop at the end. Trim the wires. Attach the beaded head pins to the necklace in the following sequence (starting from the center, working left): silver, red jasper, gold. Repeat the pattern on the other side, ending with a silver bead on each side.

6 Attach the lobster clasp set on the ends of the chain.

**MATERIALS**

Decorative paper
2 rectangular pieces of glass,
    1 x ¾ inches
Copper foil tape
Lead-free solder
4 gold-tone jump rings
4 inches of 22-gauge,
    gold-tone wire
8 mm x 12 mm red jasper
    briolette
5 round gold beads, 2 mm
Gold-tone eye pin
8 gold-tone head pins
6 silver beads
4 round red jasper beads, 3 mm
16 inches of gold-tone chain
Gold-tone lobster clasp set

# Chapter 5

# Simple Shaped Glass Projects

Smaller pieces of glass and rounded shapes can be particularly challenging to cut and solder. The projects in this chapter have been designed to help you get the knack of working with odd shapes. The skills you hone now will help you breeze through more intricate projects later in the book.

# A Graceful Update

*Giving a forgotten piece of jewelry a dazzling new focal point is one of the many advantages of working with soldered glass. Here, a matching pendant is worked into an existing necklace and briolette for added charm.*

**INSTRUCTIONS**

1 Purchase a necklace with a briolette, or look around for an old one that could use a little updating. Choose the necklace first, then find paper to match its beads and briolette.

2 Cut the paper to fit between the glass. Place the paper between the glass pieces.

3 Wrap the edges with the copper foil tape.

4 Solder the edges of the oval glass.

5 Attach jump rings to the top and bottom of the oval.

6 Temporarily remove the briolette bead from the center. Place the soldered oval in place of the briolette. Reattach the briolette to the bottom jump ring of the oval.

**MATERIALS**

Premade necklace
    with briolette(a pair-
    shaped or oval gem)
2 pieces of oval glass,
    1¼ x ¾ inch
Decorative paper
Copper foil tape
Lead-free solder
2 jump rings

# Porcelain Piece Chokers

*Turn broken or discarded pieces of porcelain into fun and colorful fashion pick-me-ups. The colors and textures you can find in craft shops—or (oops!) in your kitchen—offer almost limitless possibilities.*

## MATERIALS

Pieces of polished or
  unpolished porcelain
Copper foil tape
Lead-free solder
2 jump rings
2 strands of satin cord,
  14 inches long
2 large-hole sterling
  silver beads
2 coil ends
Lobster clasp set
Large-hole chain tab

## INSTRUCTIONS

1 Recycle broken porcelain pieces, or shape pieces for jewelry from fragments of broken china. Use a rotary tool to shape the pieces and to smooth any sharp or jagged edges.

2 Wrap the edges with the copper foil tape.

3 Solder the edges.

4 Based on your design, solder jump rings on the appropriate corners.

5 Thread the satin cord through the jump ring(s). Make a knot close to the jump ring.

6 Slide a large sterling silver bead onto both cords.

7 Thread the ends of the cords though a coil end. Squeeze the coil end down tightly to secure the cord in place.

8 Attach a lobster clasp to one coil end and a chain tab to the other end.

# Cropped Circle Choker

*Cutting your own glass opens a world of design opportunities. With a couple of basic cuts, the circular glass in this project becomes a uniquely shaped focal point.*

## INSTRUCTIONS

1 Use a marker to draw the cutting lines onto the glass circle. Trace the pattern found on page 143 directly onto the glass.

2 Cut the glass (see page 22).

3 Trim the paper to fit between the pieces of glass. Sandwich the paper and glass together.

4 Wrap the edges with the copper foil tape.

5 Solder the edges.

6 Use a large-hole sterling bead as the bail. Hold the bead on the top edge of the pendant and solder into place.

7 Thread the pendant onto the choker wire. Some chokers come with removable end beads; they simply screw off and back on. If you use one of these, replace the end bead, securing it with glue.

## MATERIALS

2 circular pieces of glass,
   1½ inches across
Decorative paper
Copper foil tape
Lead-free solder
Large-hole sterling silver bead
Prepurchased memory wire
   choker
Glue (optional)

# Cut Out for Fun

## MATERIALS

Piece of circular glass,
    2 inches across
Decorative paper
Copper foil tape
Lead-free solder
Wide nickel wire
Ball chain

*The playful shape of this project is accentuated by the colorful pattern of paper chosen to go in it. It's the perfect piece for a day at the beach or a night on the town.*

## INSTRUCTIONS

1 Cut the circle of glass into four quarters. You can use the template found on page 143 if you like. Lay the glass on the template and draw your cutting lines.

2 Cut the glass apart.

3 Trim the paper to fit between the glass. Place the paper between the glass.

4 Wrap the edges with the copper foil tape.

5 Solder the edges.

6 To make the bail, use a piece of wide nickel wire and form it into a U shape. Keep in mind the size of chain. Place each end of the open U on the front and back sides, at the point of the pie. Solder in place.

7 Clean and finish the piece with finishing wax (see page 34). Place the pendant on a ball chain, go out, and have fun.

# Classic Pearl Choker

*Make this elegant choker, and you'll see the incredible creative potential in engraving your own glass.*

**MATERIALS**

Circular piece of glass, 1 inch
    across
Copper foil tape
Lead-free solder
6 inches of 24-gauge wire
6 strands of bead wire,
    8 inches long
12 silver crimp beads
Minimum of 200 pearls, 4 mm
6 three-strand spacer bars
2 loop-end connectors
Lobster clasp set
Piece of jewelry chain,
    2 inches long
3 jump rings
Daisy spacer bead
Head pin

## INSTRUCTIONS

1 Create an etched piece of glass: Secure the round glass on a clean work surface. Use a rotary tool (see page 14) with a diamond bit to engrave an image on the glass. You can use the design in figure 1 as a template, or create a design of your own.

2 Apply copper foil tape around the edges. Make sure both sides are even and that the foil edge on the back isn't visible from the front of the piece.

3 Solder the edges of the glass.

4 Make three loops in a 3-inch piece of the 24-gauge wire (see figure 2). Trim the excess wire. Curve the triple-looped wire to fit the curve of the glass. Make two of these.

5 Place one of the triple-looped wires on the back side of the glass. Use a clamp to hold it in place.

6 Apply flux to the wire and tack solder it in place (see page 30). Repeat this for the other side (see figure 3).

7 Thread bead wire through each loop on the glass piece. Secure each with a crimp bead. Add pearls and spacer bars to each side, making sure both sides are mirror images of each other.

8 When you're done threading pearls and spacer bars, use crimp beads to secure the ends of the wires to the end connectors.

9 Add the lobster clasp to one end. On the other end, use a jump ring to attach the 2-inch piece of jewelry chain (this acts as a length extender, if needed).

10 The finishing touch: string one pearl, the daisy spacer bead, and another pearl onto a head pin. Make a loop at the top of the head pin. Attach it to the extension chain as an elegant final detail.

*Figure 1*

*Figure 2*

*Figure 3*

# Three Times the Charm

*Creating variations on a theme is a great way to get more mileage from your ideas. Once you make the basic piece in this trio of necklaces, you'll move easily through its more ornate versions.*

## Necklace with Five Bead Dangles

(SHOWN IN CENTER)

**INSTRUCTIONS**

1. Cut the paper to fit between the pieces of glass. Sandwich the paper between the glass.

2. Wrap the edges with the copper foil tape.

3. Solder the edges.

4. Solder a jump ring to the top and bottom of the pendant.

5. Make five bead dangles: string five beads onto five separate head pins. Make a loop at the top of each. Attach all five dangles to the pendant's bottom jump ring.

6. Attach the pendant to the chain with a jump ring.

7. Attach the lobster clasp set to the ends of the chain.

**MATERIALS**

Decorative paper
2 pieces of rectangular glass, 1 x ¾ inch
Copper foil tape
Lead-free solder
3 jump rings
5 head pins
5 beads of various shapes, sizes, and colors
Silver link chain, 24 inches long
Lobster clasp set

# Diamond-Shaped Pendant

## MATERIALS

Decorative paper

2 pieces of diamond-shaped glass, 1½ x ¾ inch

Copper foil tape

Lead-free solder

Strand of link chain, 22 inches long

2 inches of 20-gauge wire

12 head pins

Eye pin

7 flat round beads, 4 mm

7 green bicone beads, 5 mm

Lobster clasp set

## INSTRUCTIONS

1 Cut the paper to fit between the pieces of glass. Place the paper between the glass. If you need to cut the diamond shape glass yourself, there's a pattern on page 143 that you may find handy.

2 Wrap the edges with the copper foil tape.

3 Solder the edges.

4 Cut the 20-gauge wire into two pieces. Bend each into a small U shape.

5 Solder the U-shaped pieces of wire onto the top and bottom points of the diamond.

6 Slide one flat round bead onto the eye pin and make a loop at the other end (see page 36). Attach this dangle to the top of the diamond pendant. Attach the pendant to the center of the chain.

7 Create 12 dangles with the remaining head pins and beads. Make loops at each end and trim the ends of the wire. Attach one bicone bead to the bottom of the pendant.

Attach the other bead dangles to the chain starting five links out from the center and alternating the beads. Continue the pattern with five links between each bead dangle.

8 Attach the lobster clasp set on the ends of the chain.

74

# Rectangular Pendant with Briolette

## INSTRUCTIONS

1 Cut the paper to fit between the pieces of glass. Place the paper between the glass.

2 Wrap the edges with the copper foil tape.

3 Solder the edges.

4 Solder one jump ring to the top and bottom of the pendant.

5 Cut off 1 inch of the silver link chain. Use a jump ring to attach it to the other jump ring on top of the pendant. Attach the pendant to the center of the chain.

6 String the wire through the briolette. Wrap the top of the wire into a loop. Attach the briolette to the bottom jump ring of the pendant.

7 Use head pins to make the remaining beads into dangles. Finish each with a loop, and trim the ends.

8 Attach one small bead to the bottom of the pendant.

9 Attach six dangles to the short piece of chain at the top of the pendant (from step 5).

10 Attach the rest of the bead dangles onto the necklace close to the pendant.

11 Attach the lobster clasp set to the ends of the chain.

## MATERIALS

Decorative paper
2 pieces of rectangular glass, 1½ x ½ inch
Copper foil tape
Lead-free solder
4 jump rings
Silver link chain, 20 inches long
Large briolette
3 inches of 24-gauge wire
17 head pins
17 beads of various shapes, colors, and sizes
Lobster clasp set

# Turquoise Cabochon Jewelry

*For a slight change of pace, try wrapping and soldering various types of polished stones. The silver solder and wire bring out the natural beauty of all types of stones, as seen in this group of turquoise pieces.*

## Turquoise Neck Cuff

**INSTRUCTIONS**

1 Cover the back of each cabochon with the copper foil tape. Wrap the edges of each cabochon. The upper edge of the tape should meet the uppermost crest of the stone's edge. Burnish the tape thoroughly.

2 Solder the copper foiled edges and backs of each stone.

3 Cut a piece of the wire long enough to back all three cabochons put together. Add an extra ½ inch to the length. This piece of wire will serve as the base wire for the three cabochons. Bend the top end of the wire into a loop (make sure the loop remains large enough to go over the neck cuff later in the process). Solder the loop shut.

4 Use a clamp to hold the smallest cabochon onto the base wire right below the loop, center it, and solder it into place. Clamp the medium cabochon below the first one, center it, and solder it into place. Place the largest stone below the medium cabochon, center it, and solder it into place.

5 Cover the base wire and back of the cabochons completely with solder so that the surface is smooth.

6 Use the finishing technique of your choice to smooth the soldered surface (see page 33).

**MATERIALS**

3 oval turquoise cabochons
    of different sizes
Copper foil tape
Lead-free solder
Heavy-gauge wire
2 jump rings
Lobster clasp

# Turquoise Ring

### INSTRUCTIONS

1 Cover the back of the cabochon with the copper foil tape. Wrap the copper foil tape around edges.

2 Solder the back and edges of the stone.

3 Solder one end of the wire to the middle of the back of the cabochon.

4 String the beads onto the wire.

5 Wrap the beaded wire around your finger to size it correctly. Be sure to size it after stringing the beads onto the wire.

6 Trim the wire, but be sure to leave enough so you can solder it onto the back of the cabochon.

7 Solder the end of the wire in place. Keep the solder smooth. Be sure to coat the wire completely to make it comfortable on your finger.

8 Smooth the soldered surfaces with the finishing technique of your choice (see page 35).

7 Cut a piece of the heavy-gauge wire long enough to fit around your neck like a choker. Add an extra inch to this length.

8 Slide the triple cabochon pendant onto the wire. Bend each end into a loop.

9 Bend the heavy-gauge wire into a circle that is large enough to fit around your neck.

10 Use the jump rings to attach the lobster clasp to the ends of the wire.

### MATERIALS

Turquoise cabochon
Copper foil tape
Lead-free solder
4 inches of 18-gauge wire
Sterling silver beads

# Turquoise Wrist Cuff

**INSTRUCTIONS**

1 Wrap the copper foil tape around each cabochon. The upper edge of the tape should meet the uppermost crest of the stone's edge. Burnish the tape thoroughly.

2 Solder the copper foiled edges of each stone.

3 Cut the wire at an angle. Solder one end to the edge of the larger stone. Solder over the angled end of the wire for a smooth transition between the cabochon and the wire. Set the piece aside and let it get completely cool.

4 Hold the piece firmly where the wire joins the stone, and bend the wire into a loose curve around the cabochon.

5 Curve the remaining portion of wire into a spiral shape that comfortably fits around your wrist.

6 Solder the other end of the wire to the edge of the smaller cabochon. Let it cool.

7 Hold the piece firmly where the wire joins the stone. Carefully bend the wire into a loose oval around the cabochon.

8 Bend and form the cuff as needed to fit.

**MATERIALS**

2 oval turquoise cabochons of slightly different sizes
Copper foil tape
Lead-free solder
10 inches of 16-gauge silver wire

# Flat Marble Necklace and Earrings

*Unusually shaped glass is great to use in jewelry because it tends to play wonderful tricks with light. In this project, flat glass marbles act like magnifying lenses for the images behind them. See what visual treats you can concoct after a trip to a craft store or bead shop.*

## INSTRUCTIONS

1 Use a favorite rubber stamp to create an image or graphic design onto the paper. Be sure to use black permanent ink.

2 Cut the paper to fit the circular pieces of glass.

3 Cover the back of the paper with the foil tape. Trim the excess tape from the paper's edge.

4 Place the foiled paper, image side first, against a glass marble. Wrap copper foil tape around the edges, having more foil extending toward the back. Make sure no paper is showing from the edge of the foil tape. Burnish in place.

5 Solder the back side of each marble first. Let the solder set. Sometimes little pits appear in the solder; this is usually caused from adhesive that oozes up through the solder. Let it cool, and scrape off the adhesive pits. Apply flux to the pits and more solder to fill them, if needed.

6 Once the backs are soldered, solder around the front edges of the copper, blending the solder together to make it smooth.

## MATERIALS

White paper
Graphically interesting
  rubber stamp
Black permanent ink pad
Large flat glass marble
2 small flat glass marbles
Copper foil tape, ½ inch wide
Lead-free solder
12 inches of 20-gauge wire
Black patina
2 ball-head pins
15 inches of black suede lace,
  3 mm wide
2 fold-over crimps
2 small jump rings
Large jump ring
Lobster clasp

7 To make the loops at the top edges of the pieces, twist the wire together forming a loop with a long tail. Clip the twisted wire end at the base of the twist. Bend the long tail of wire that is left into a spiral (See figure 1).

8 Place the twisted end on the top edge of each marble, and solder in place. Bend the spiral to lie flat against the marble.

9 To make the decorative spirals at the bottom of the marbles, form the spirals first. At the end of each spiral, make a small right-angle bend (see figure 2). Solder the spirals (at the right-angle bend) to the bottom center edge.

10 Clean all flux and residue from the marbles and wires.

11 Place the marbles onto a paper plate, and paint all the wires and soldered surfaces with the patina (see page 35).

12 Once all the patina coats are dry, rinse each piece with water. Let them dry completely before applying finishing wax (see page 34).

13 If you don't have a set of purchased ear wires, you can make them easily from a couple of head pins. Here's how: Create a small loop at the ball end of the pin. Form a long U shape with the other end. Add a small angle bend at the end of the pin. Slide the charms onto the ball end of the ear wire. Bend the ball end in to close the loop.

14 To make the necklace, cut the suede to length. Slide large marble charm onto the necklace. Attach the fold-over crimps to the ends of the suede. Attach jump rings and the lobster clasp.

*Figure 1*

*Figure 2*

# Chapter 6

# Embellishing Soldered Jewelry Pieces

*In this chapter, you'll learn how easy it is to enhance jewelry and soldered charms by using (and sometimes re-using) bead wire and small metal objects. My only advice? Experiment and explore. Have fun with the materials and follow your creative instincts.*

# Beautiful Bobby Pins

*Who says ordinary items should be boring? Here's an idea that uses some basic soldering techniques to brighten up simple bobby pins. Wear them in your hair, use them as a bookmark, or attach them to other craft projects.*

## MATERIALS

Group of metal bobby pins
Lead-free solder
Decorative metal box corner
Small turquoise cabochon
Copper foil tape
Flower brad
Metal decorative brads
Metal button
Decorative toggle clasp

### INSTRUCTIONS

1 Sand off any plastic coating or paint from the bobby pin. This will expose the metal underneath.

2 Flux the sanded spot, then melt a small amount of solder onto that spot.

## Decorative Metal Corner

1 Cut apart the decorative metal box corner so that you have just one long piece to use.

2 Flux the concave back side and melt solder to fill it (see page 33).

3 Lay the bobby pin on the back side and re-melt the solder that is on the decorative piece so that it flows onto the bobby pin. The bobby pin will get hot, so use pliers to hold it.

# Turquoise Cabochon

1 Wrap the cabochon with the copper foil tape, completely covering the back. Flux and solder.

2 Solder the bobby pin to the back side.

# Decorative Brads

1 Cut off the legs of a brad.

2 Flux the back of the brad, and melt solder onto the fluxed area.

3 Solder onto the bobby pin.

# Metal Button

1 Cut the shank off the back of the button.

2 Flux the button's back, and melt solder onto the fluxed area.

3 Solder the button to the bobby pin.

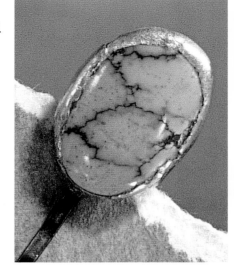

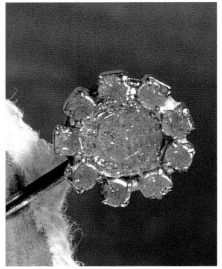

# Decorative Toggle Clasp

1 Remove the toggle shank.

2 Flux the back of the clasp, and melt solder onto the fluxed area.

3 Solder it to the bobby pin.

# Beaded Necklace and Bracelet

Take two basic soldered charms, add some wire, practice your beading skills for a moment, and presto! You'll get an amazingly charming necklace and bracelet set.

## MATERIALS

4 pieces of glass, 1 x ¾ inch
Decorative paper
Copper foil tape
Lead-free solder
20-gauge wire
8 jump rings
17 pink beads, 6 mm
58 pink beads, 2 mm
53 clear beads, 4 mm
3 head pins
30 inches of bead wire
12 crimp tubes
64 pink seed beads, 3 mm
Toggle clasp

# Beaded Necklace

### INSTRUCTIONS

1 Trim the paper to fit between the pieces of glass. Put the paper and glass together.

2 Wrap the edges with the copper foil tape.

3 Solder all the edges.

4 Create a set of three, triple-looped wires. Start with a piece of wire 3 inches in length. Make a loop in the center of the wire. Line up the loop with the center of the glass charm. Mark the wire for the location of the other two loops. Make the two loops.

5 Trim the ends of the wire.

6 Use a clamp to hold the wire in place. Tack solder the wire to the glass charms (see page 30).

7 Solder on a top jump ring to the necklace charm.

8 Make three bead dangles: thread pink beads and clear beads onto a head pin and make a loop a the top. Attach bead charms to the bottom edge.

9 Cut a piece of bead wire 18 inches in length. Make a loop and use a crimp tube to secure one end. String on beads starting with the seed beads. String on 32 seed beads (using seed beads on the ends of the necklace is an inexpensive way to add length to a necklace).

10 String on a 2 mm pink bead, a 4 mm clear bead, and a 6 mm pink bead. Repeat this pattern until the seventh 6 mm pink bead is on. Add another 6 mm pink bead. The charm will be attached to the necklace between the two 6 mm beads. Continue the pattern as before, ending when the seventh 2 mm pink bead is on. String on 32 seed beads to the end of the wire. Finish with a crimp tube, leaving a small loop at the end.

11 Attach the toggle clasp set to the two end loops using jump rings.

# Beaded Bracelet

### INSTRUCTIONS

1 Trim matching paper to fit between the pieces of glass. Put the paper and glass together.

2 Wrap the edges with the copper foil tape.

3 Solder all the edges.

4 Cut six pieces of bead wire, 3 inches in length. Use a crimp tube to secure one end, leaving a small loop. Do this for all six strands.

5 For each of the four outside strands, start with one 2 mm pink bead, then one 4 mm clear bead. Alternate the beads until the strand is long enough to fit your wrist (approximately 16 beads). Add a crimp tube to secure.

6 For the center bead strands, start the strand with a clear bead, then alternate with pink beads. Once the strand is long enough, add one 6 mm pink bead; follow with one clear 4 mm bead and one pink 2 mm bead. Finish each strand by making a loop and securing it with a crimp tube.

7 At the end of the bead strands, connect the three strands together with a jump ring threaded through the loops. Attach the toggle clasp set to the ends.

# Framed Memories Pendant

*A whimsical use of a free-formed wire can make a simple pendant come to life and help frame special memories in a wonderfully artistic way. If you have a digital camera and computer, or access to a copier, experiment with reducing photos to sizes you can use for jewelry projects like this one.*

**INSTRUCTIONS**

1 Trim the photo to fit the glass. Position it between the pieces of glass.

2 Wrap the edges with the copper foil tape.

3 Solder all the edges.

4 Lay the charm flat on your work surface. Work with the wire to form it into a creative shape around the edges of the glass. Be sure to extend part of the wire design above the top of the charm so you can thread the cord through it.

5 Use a clamp to hold the wire in place. Flux and tack solder into place (see page 30).

6 Thread the leather cord through the wire at the top. Thread both ends through one silver bead, one glass bead, and one silver bead. Slide the beads down close to the coil. The beads should hold the pendant in place.

7 Tie the ends of the leather cord together in a knot.

**NOTE:** When using photography, be sure to use a non-glossy photographic paper. It's preferable to use one that's heat and moisture resistant.

**MATERIALS**

2 pieces of glass, 1 inch square
Small black and white photograph
Copper foil tape
Lead-free solder
3 inches of 26-gauge silver wire
24 inches of 1 mm leather cord
2 large-hole silver beads
Large-hole glass bead

# Daisy Pendant and Earrings

*Adding ornate bars from disassembled toggle clasps lets you "frame" the subject of your glass pieces in interesting ways, as seen here in this sunny and cheerful earring and pendant set.*

## INSTRUCTIONS

1 Trim the paper to fit between the glass pieces. Sandwich the glass and paper together.

2 Wrap all the edges with the copper foil tape.

3 Solder all the edges.

4 Disassemble the toggle bar clasps. You'll use the toggle bars from each set as a decorative edge on the glass pieces. Prepare them by using wire cutters to remove the loops from three of the toggle bars.

5 Flux the toggle bars. Use a clamp to hold the toggle bars in place. Tack solder one bar to the top and one bar to the bottom of each charm (see page 30). Use the toggle bars with a loop (from step 4) on the top of the charms.

6 For the earrings, place one daisy bead on a head pin and create a loop at the other end (see page 36). Attach one loop to the glass charm. Attach the other loop to an ear wire.

7 Thread the bead wire through the loop on the pendant charm. Center the wire on the loop. Thread both wire ends through a daisy bead.

8 Begin threading beads onto each wire. Alternate one glass bead and one silver bead until the fifth glass bead is on: then thread one silver daisy bead. Repeat this pattern to the end of the wire. Make sure both wires mirror each other.

9 Secure the ends with a crimp bead, leaving a small loop at the ends.

10 Attach the lobster clasp set to the loops on the ends of the wire.

## MATERIALS

Decorative paper
2 pieces of glass, $1\frac{1}{2}$ x $\frac{1}{2}$ inch
4 pieces of glass, 1 x $\frac{1}{2}$ inch
Copper foil tape
Lead-free solder
6 toggle bars (from toggle clasp sets)
9 silver daisy beads
Head pin
2 ear wires
19 inches of bead wire
60 glass beads, 5 mm
48 round silver beads, 3 mm
2 crimp beads
Lobster clasp set

# Oval Neck Cuff and Earrings

*Silver floral add-ons give these playful pink ovals a bright, classic look.*

## MATERIALS

Decorative paper

4 pieces of oval glass, $\frac{3}{4}$ x $\frac{1}{2}$ inch

2 pieces of oval glass, $1\frac{1}{4}$ X $\frac{3}{4}$ inch

Copper foil tape

Lead-free solder

Piece of 3 mm half-round nickel wire, $\frac{3}{4}$ inch in length

2 medium decorative toggle clasps

Large decorative toggle clasp

13 inches of 2 mm square nickel wire

2 ball head pins

## INSTRUCTIONS

1 Cut the paper to fit the glass pieces. Fit the paper and glass pieces together.

2 Wrap the edges with the copper foil tape.

3 Solder the edges of each piece.

4 To form the bail for the pendant, bend the half-round wire into a U shape. Squeeze the open end of the U together to close the bail. Flux the bail, and solder it onto the top edge of the oval pendant.

5 Cut off the connector loops from the backs of the toggle sets. Smooth off any rough edges or bumps with a file or rotary tool.

6 Clamp the flourishes onto the pendant and earrings. Flux the contact points and solder them into place.

7 Create the neck cuff by bending the square nickel wire into a large C shape. Use a coffee can or other round object to shape the wire. Curve the wire so that the front comes down on the chest and the back end wires curve down at the back of the neck. Add a bead of solder to the ends (where the wire was cut) for a smooth end. Slide on the oval pendant.

8 To make the ear wires, take a ball head pin and make a small loop at the end. Form a long U shape with the other end. Add a small angle bend toward the end of the pin. Slide an oval earring charm onto the ball end of the ear wire. Bend the ball end in to close the loop. Repeat this process for the second earring.

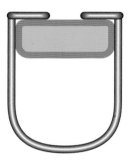

*Figure 1*

# Spiral Wire Bead Ring

**INSTRUCTIONS**

1 Wrap the copper foil tape around the outer edges of the glass bead. Trim the foil tape as needed.

2 Solder the foiled edges of the bead.

3 Form the ring by wrapping the wire on a ring mandrel. Create a U shape. If you do not have a ring mandrel, wrap the wire around your finger to get the correct size, then bend the wire around a cylindrical shape (like a glue stick) to help refine the shape.

4 Make a spiral on each end of the wire (see page 37). When making the spirals, bend them so that they're turned out in opposite directions of each other.

5 Bend the spiral ends at a 90° angle over the top of the bead (see figure 1). Adjust the spirals to lie flat on top of the bead.

6 Use a clamp to hold the wire in place. Flux the wire that touches the soldered edge.

7 Melt solder to the wire to tack it in place.

**MATERIALS**

Large square glass bead
Copper foil tape
Lead-free solder
3 to 4 inches of 20-gauge wire
Ring mandrel

# Tapestry Collection

Using woven fabric can evoke the qualities of bygone eras, even conjuring images of tapestry-lined halls or an ancient family crest. The half oval cuts of glass and adorning beadwork on these pieces serve to accentuate this nostalgic mood.

# Triple Charm Necklace

**INSTRUCTIONS**

1 Cut the glass ovals and mirrors in half. Use the template on page 143 if you need help drawing accurate cut lines.

2 Trim the ribbon to the size of the pieces of glass. Fit the ribbon between the glass and mirror pieces. Make sure the mirror side is facing out.

3 Wrap each piece with the copper foil tape. Solder all the edges.

4 Lie one of the charms facedown. Center the chain on the top edge of the charm. Make sure the links of the chain are flat against the back. Flux and solder the chain into place.

5 Lay the next charm facedown and space it five links of the chain to the right of the first charm. Make sure the chain is not twisted. The links should line up and lay flat. Flux and solder the chain into place.

6 Repeat this process with the third charm, spacing it five links to the left of the first charm. Flux and solder the last charm into place.

7 Use head pins to make bead dangles. You'll need eight dangles with one gold bead, five dangles with three gold beads, and 10 dangles with one red bead.

8 Starting on one side of the three charms, attach five bead dangles in this order: single gold bead dangle; single red bead dangle; triple gold bead dangle; single red bead dangle; and one single bead gold dangle. Follow this pattern until the spaces between and next to the charms are filled. Attach each bead dangle to its own link of chain. No jump rings are needed.

9 Finish one end of the chain with two single red bead dangles and one triple gold bead dangle. Attach the lobster clasp set to the ends.

# Matching Earrings

**INSTRUCTIONS**

1 Use two of the remaining half oval charms created in steps 1 through 4 of the necklace.

2 Solder two small jump rings onto the corners of both charms.

3 Cut the toggle clasps apart. Use the part of the design that best fits along the straight edge of the cut ovals.

4 Use a clamp to hold the piece in place. Tack solder the toggle piece into place (see page 30). Blend the metal edges together by fluxing and adding solder.

5 Cut four pieces of chain, ¾ inch long each. Attach two of the chains to each charm and earring post.

**MATERIALS**

3 pieces of oval glass, 1 x ¾ inch

3 oval mirrors, 1 x ¾ inch

Woven ribbon or fabric

Copper foil tape

Lead-free solder

18 inches of silver link chain

27 head pins

24 gold seed beads, 3 mm

10 red beads, 4 mm

Lobster clasp set

6 small jump rings

2 decorative silver toggle clasps

4 inches of silver chain

2 earring posts

# Ornate Pendant

### INSTRUCTIONS

1 Cut the oval glass and oval mirror in half.

2 Cut the ribbon to fit between the glass pieces. Sandwich the ribbon between the glass and mirror (mirror side facing out).

3 Wrap the edges with silver-backed copper foil tape. Solder all the edges.

4 Starting at the center of the round edge, solder on one small jump ring. Continue soldering on jump rings until 13 are soldered onto the edge.

5 Cut the loop off of the backside of the large toggle bar. Use a clamp to hold the bar along the top edge of the pendant. Flux and tack solder it into place.

6 Place the pendant facedown. Lay two small jump rings on the upper corners of the pendant and solder them into place. Be sure to attach the jump rings with the open side facing out so you can open them later to attach the chain.

7 Attach 10 inches of chain to each corner's jump ring.

8 Make a center connector for the chain using one eye pin. String on one gold bead, one red bead, and one gold bead. Make a loop on the end and trim off the excess wire.

Attach the ends of the connector to each side of the chain about six links up from the pendant. Attach the lobster clasp set to the ends.

9 Use seven head pins to make four gold bead dangles and three red bead dangles for the bottom edge of the pendant.

10 Attach one gold bead dangle to the first jump ring. Skip a jump ring and attach a red bead dangle to the next jump ring. Continue alternating until the last jump ring has a gold bead dangle attached.

11 Cut three 2-inch pieces of chain. Use small jump rings to attach the chain lengths. Attach the first chain onto the second jump ring down. Attach the other end of the chain to the sixth jump ring over (see figure 1). Attach the second chain to the fourth jump ring down. Attach the other end to the sixth jump ring over. Attach the last chain on the sixth jump ring down, attach the other end six jump rings over.

*Figure 1*

### MATERIALS

Oval glass 2 x 1½ inches
Oval mirror 2 x 1½ inches
1-inch wide decorative ribbon
Silver-backed copper foil tape
Lead-free solder
19 small jump rings
1 large decorative toggle bar
26 inches of small link silver chain
1 eye pin
10 gold seed beads
4 red oval facet glass beads, 4 mm
Lobster clasp set
7 head pins

99

# Chapter 7

# Soldered Fusion: Building Impact by Combining Pieces

*In this chapter, you'll see how easy it is to make interesting and more complex pieces of jewelry by combining individual soldered pieces. You can join pieces together using beads, findings, jump rings, or chain, or simply solder pieces to each other. As you create your own designs, think about color, play around with shapes, and see where the muse leads.*

# Mosaic Pendant

Take miniature versions of your favorite paintings or photographs and give them your own artistic interpretation by fusing them together in a truly unique way. Here, three separate soldered charms were pieced together to make a fun and distinct pendant.

## INSTRUCTIONS

1 Make color copies of your favorite paintings and photographs, or use pictures clipped from a catalog or magazine. If you have access to a computer or copier, reduce the size to fit the sizes of glass. Trim the copies to fit under each piece of glass.

2 Cut the cardboard to fit the back of each piece. Cover the cardboard with aluminum tape.

3 Sandwich the pictures between the glass and the aluminum-covered cardboard.

4 Wrap the edges with the copper foil tape.

5 Solder all the edges of each piece.

6 Lay the pieces flat, facedown. Tack solder the pieces together by melting little drops of solder on the seams where they line up.

7 Add more solder and melt the seams together.

8 Turn the piece over and melt the seams together on the front side to form one seam. Add extra solder to create a "bead" along the seams (see page 28).

9 Pry apart the silver bell bead charms and place them on each corner of the pendant at an angle. Squeeze them together and clamp them into place. Flux and tack solder them in place.

10 Cut a piece of cord 5 inches long. Thread it through one ring on the bell bead charm and fold it in half. Bring the ends together and string on 10 orange beads. Tie a knot to secure the end. Don't tie the knot too close to the beads. Leave some room for the next step. Repeat this for the other side's bell bead charm.

11 Cut two pieces of hemp, 24 inches long. Thread the strands between the last orange bead and the knot on the hemp strands from step 10. Bring the ends together. There should now be four strands. Repeat this on the other side.

12 Coat the knot and the four strands by the knot with clear drying glue. Let it stand until it's tacky. Cut a 4-inch long piece of hemp and wrap it around the knot and the strands. Clip the ends, and glue in place to secure. Repeat this process for the other side.

13 On the end of one set of strands, fold the ends over to form a loop. At the base of the loop, apply more glue and let it stand until it's tacky. Cut a 4-inch piece of hemp and wrap it around all the strands. Trim the ends, and secure with glue. Trim any ends that may be hanging out.

14 On the other set of strands, string a strand through the button shank and fold it over. Fold the other three strands down to match. Apply clear glue around all the strands, and let it stand until tacky. Cut a 4-inch piece of hemp and wrap it around all the strands. Trim the ends, and secure with glue.

## MATERIALS

Copies of paintings, color pictures, or other art
Piece of glass, ½ inch square
Piece of glass, ½ x ¾ inch
Piece of glass, 1 x ¾ inch
Cardboard
Aluminum tape
Copper foil tape
Lead-free solder
2 silver bell bead charms
90 inches of white hemp bead cord
20 orange, large-hole donut beads, 7 mm
Clear drying glue
Silver shank-backed button

# Soldered "Dancing" Figurine

*With a little ingenuity and a sense of humor, you can create charming and whimsical pieces, such as this vintage-looking dancing figurine.*

## MATERIALS

Piece of glass, 1 inch square

Piece of glass, 2 inches square

Piece of round glass, 1 inch across

Festive paper

Photograph of a face

Corset clip art

Scrap piece of aluminum

Copper foil tape

Lead-free solder

Decorative metal crown

Piece of jewelry with curved flourishes

Small metal connector

4 small jump rings

Medium metal connector

Large metal connector

Pair of arm charms

Pair of leg charms

2 head pins

2 daisy spacer beads

2 red glass flower beads

Large jump ring

Ribbon

## INSTRUCTIONS

1 Cut both square pieces of glass in half, corner to corner, to create triangles.

2 Trim the paper and photos to fit the circle and triangles. Use a close up of a face for the circular piece. Cut paper triangles for the triangular pieces of glass. Use the corset clip art in the smaller triangle for the upper body of the doll.

3 In this project, the top of a cocoa container was used for the scrap piece of aluminum. Aluminum was used because solder doesn't stick to it. Trim the aluminum to fit the glass piece.

4 Sandwich the face photo between the glass and the piece of aluminum. Wrap the edge of the circle with the copper foil tape. Fit the triangular pieces of glass and paper together. Wrap the edges of the triangles with the copper foil tape.

5 Solder the edges of the circle and triangles.

6 The crown in this example is brass. It was "tinned" to make it silver (see page 32). To create the hair, curved flourishes were cut from a piece of jewelry. They were left brass-colored to contrast with the silver crown.

**13** Connect the head to the upper body with a beaded head pin. Thread one daisy spacer and one red flower bead onto a head pin. Slip the head pin through the head connector and the upper body connector. Bend the head pin at a right angle up toward the head. Solder the end of the head pin to the base of the head. Make sure the pieces can swing freely.

**14** Connect the lower body to the upper body, as in step 13, by threading one daisy spacer and one red flower bead onto a head pin. Slip the head pin through the upper body connector and the lower body connector. Bend the head pin at a right angle up toward the upper body. Solder the end of the head pin to the base of the upper body.

**15** Connect the arm and leg charms.

**16** Solder one large jump ring onto the back side of the head behind the crown. Thread ribbon through the jump-ring to hang the doll.

**7** Use a small clamp to hold the crown to the top of the glass circle. Flux the back part of the crown and tack solder it in place (see page 30).

**8** Use a small clamp to hold the flourishes in place. Flux the back side and solder them into place.

**9** Solder a small connector at the base of the circular piece for the neck attachment.

**10** On the long straight edge of the 1-inch-wide triangle, solder a small jump ring. On the point opposite the jump ring, solder

the medium connector so that the hole is at the pointed end.

**11** On the outer corners of the triangle just below the points, solder on a small jump ring at each side. Leave the opening of the jump rings facing toward the back so you can open them and slip on the arm charms.

**12** On the 2-inch-wide triangle, solder the larger connector to the top center point. Solder two jump rings along the bottom edge towards the center, but leave a space between them so the leg charms will dangle freely.

# Triple Strand Transformation

*Mastering even the most basic soldering and beading skills opens up a world of possibilities for updating almost anything. In this case, a simple necklace was reborn as a triple-strand necklace when soldered glass charms were added to the ends.*

**INSTRUCTIONS**

1 Trim the paper to fit the glass pieces. Place the paper between the glass.

2 Wrap the edges of the pieces with the copper foil tape. Solder all the edges.

3 Cut the two loops off the bottom edge of the connectors with heavy wire cutters. Solder the connectors to the top edge of each charm.

4 Solder three small jump rings on the bottom edge of each charm, spacing them evenly apart.

5 Cut a length of silver link chain 8 inches long. Attach the ends of the chain to the innermost soldered jump rings.

6 Attach five black briolettes and four smoky-clear briolettes to the chain with small jump rings. Space them evenly by measuring or counting the links between them.

7 Cut 9 inches of silver link chain. Attach the ends to the middle jump ring on each charm.

8 Cut 10 inches of silver link chain. Attach the ends to the outermost soldered jump rings on each charm.

9 Attach seven black briolettes and six smoky-clear briolettes to the chain with small jump rings. Space them evenly along the chain as in step 7.

10 Cut two 4-inch pieces of silver link chain and attach to the decorative connectors on the top edge of each charm.

11 Connect both ends of the chains to the 7-inch smaller link chain (to be used to adjust the length when needed).

**MATERIALS**

Decorative paper
4 pieces of glass, ¾ inch square
Copper foil tape
Lead-free solder
2 silver decorative connectors
28 small jump rings
35 inches of silver link chain
12 black briolettes, 8 mm x 5 mm
10 smoky-clear briolettes, 8 mm x 5 mm
7 inches of smaller silver link chain

# Colorful Daisy Brooch

*Try a technique that joins paper, glass, and copper foil tape together, and watch your creativity blossom.*

## MATERIALS

Glitter paper
6 pieces of oval glass, $\frac{3}{4}$ x $\frac{1}{2}$ inch
Piece of circular glass, $\frac{3}{4}$ inch across
Yellow ink
Copper foil tape
Lead-free solder
Nickel ball chain
Pin back

## INSTRUCTIONS

1 Cut the glitter paper to fit the oval and round pieces of glass. For the center, you can tint the white glitter paper with yellow ink.

2 Cover the back of each piece of paper with the copper foil tape.

3 Place the glass over the paper and wrap edges with the copper foil tape.

4 Coat the back with flux, and melt solder to cover the back side of each piece. Solder the edges of each piece.

5 Lay the soldered pieces facedown. Arrange the oval petals around the center.

6 Melt a small amount of solder where each oval glass makes contact with the round glass.

7 Cut the ball chain to fit around the edge of the round glass. Start on one end of the ball chain, add flux, and hold in place with tweezers. Melt solder that's already on the edge of the round glass, and tack the first ball of the chain in place. Lay the ball chain in place and solder again on the third ball over. Continue around until the ball chain is secure and the end of the ball chain is soldered into place.

8 Center the pin back on the back of the finished piece. Flux and solder in place.

# Circular Trio Pendant

*Combining circles in graduated sizes creates a uniquely bold piece that will add a stylish statement to any outfit.*

## MATERIALS

4 pieces of circular glass,
   ¾ inch across
2 pieces of circular glass, 1 inch
   across
Decorative paper
Copper foil tape
Lead-free solder
12 inches of silver link chain
16 small jump rings
7 pewter decorative connectors
Lobster clasp

**INSTRUCTIONS**

1 Cut the paper to fit between the glass pieces. Place the paper between the glass.

2 Copper foil and solder the edges of each piece.

3 Lay the pieces facedown in the order you want them to be joined together. Melt a small amount of solder at the point where the pieces contact each other.

4 Cut two 1-inch sections of chain. Attach a small jump ring to one end of the chain. Close the jump ring and solder it to the outer edge of the circles. Make sure to keep the chain away from the solder.

5 Attach the other end of the chain to a pewter connector with a small jump ring.

6 Cut four more 1-inch sections and repeat the pattern, attaching the chain to the connectors.

7 Cut two 2-inch pieces of chain for the ends.

8 Use a jump ring to attach a lobster clasp set to the ends.

# Mixed Shape Necklace

*Make an irresistibly fun necklace by stringing together charms of various sizes and shapes.*

**INSTRUCTIONS**

1  Cut the paper to fit the glass pieces. Sandwich the paper and glass pieces together.

2  Wrap the edges with the copper foil.

3  Solder all the edges.

4  Using a rotary tool with a diamond bit, sand the soldered edges to give them a brushed finish.

5  Solder two jump rings to the upper edge of the largest round glass. Use jump rings to attach 1 inch of chain to each soldered jump ring.

6  Solder two jump rings onto opposite points of the ¾-inch square. Solder two jump rings onto the ¾-inch ends of the rectangle. Attach the ends of the chains to the soldered jump rings. Cut two more 1-inch pieces of chain and attach them to the other ends.

7  Continue soldering jump rings to each charm. Connect each charm with jump rings and 1-inch pieces of chain.

8  To finish, connect longer pieces of chain to the final charms.

9  Attach the lobster clasp set to the ends of the chains.

**MATERIALS**

Decorative paper
2 pieces of round glass, 1 ⅛ inches across
2 pieces of rectangular glass, 1 x ¾ inch
2 pieces of round glass, ¾ inch across
2 pieces of rectangular glass, ¾ x ½ inch
4 pieces of glass, ¾ inch square
2 pieces of oval glass, ¾ x ½ inch
Copper foil tape
Lead-free solder
20 to 30 medium jump rings
12 inches of silver link chain
Lobster clasp set

# Sassy Daisy Wrist Cuff

*Using layers of brightly colored charms gives this leather cuff a sunny new disposition. This technique calls for the paper to be placed between one piece of glass and foil tape (instead of two pieces of glass), keeping the pieces light and stackable.*

**INSTRUCTIONS**

1   Trim the paper to fit under the glass. Apply aluminum foil tape to the back of the paper. Since the back will not be visible, use the foil tape in place of glass. Place the glass over the front of the paper.

2   Wrap the edges of all the pieces with the copper foil tape.

3   Solder the edges of all the oval charms.

4   Fan out five of the ovals facedown to create the first layer of petals. Melt solder onto the points at which the petals contact each other.

5   Repeat step 4 with the remaining five ovals.

6   Layer the two sets of petals so they're visible from the front. Tack solder the layers together where they contact each other.

7   Make a circle with the wire. Solder the ends together. Tack solder the wire onto the back side of the flower.

**MATERIALS**

Decorative paper
Aluminum foil tape
10 pieces of oval glass,
   $3/4$ x $1/2$ inch
Copper foil tape
Lead-free solder
2 inches of 30-gauge wire
Leather cuff
Thread
8 mm pink pearl
6 sage green potato pearls,
   4 mm
Fast-setting glue

8 Center the soldered flower face-up on the leather cuff. Use a marker to mark four spots under the flower where the wire touches the cuff.

9 Use the sharp point of an awl to make holes in the cuff where the pen marks are. Sew the daisy to the cuff by bringing the thread up through the bottom and over the wire, then back down through the leather cuff. Continue around until the daisy is secure. Finish off with a small knot in the thread.

10 Poke two holes in the leather in the center of the flower.

Sew on the pink pearl in the center of the flower.

11 Mark three spots at the side of the flower for the green pearls. Poke holes in the cuff, and sew the pearls onto the cuff.

12 Trim all knots on the back side of the cuff. Dot each knot with a little bit of fast-setting glue to secure.

116

# Chapter 8

# Beyond Jewelry:
## Altered Keepsakes for the Home

*Here's your chance to let your creativity shine. The art of soldering is not limited to jewelry. As you'll see, you can make many decorative and useful things out of solder and glass. You can also transform common household items into one-of-a-kind, eye-popping treasures.*

# Scrapbook Frames

*Here's a novel way to turn family photos, personal thoughts, and memories into a time capsule of creativity.*

## MATERIALS

Festive paper
4 glass panels, 2 x 3 inches each
Photos
Printed captions
Glue
Copper foil tape
Lead-free solder
Small decorative hinge
Ornate box latch

## INSTRUCTIONS

NOTE: Keep in mind that the hinges in this project will get very hot and will likely retain the heat for a while, so be careful not to touch them until they've cooled. Also, make sure you don't get flux and solder into the rotating part of the hinges. Otherwise, they'll be soldered in place and won't move.

1 Cut four paper backgrounds to fit the glass.

2 Trim the photos to fit between the glass panels.

3 Use a computer, clip art, or typewriter to generate the title and names. Glue them into place on the photos.

4 Place the cover page and the first inside page back to back. Place the back page and the second inside page back to back.

5 Wrap the edges with the copper foil tape.

6 Solder all the edges.

7 Lay the soldered pieces side by side, with the inside pages facing up. Place the hinge in the center of the pages along the soldered edge. Flux and tack solder in place (see page 30).

8 Place one side of the box latch on the center outside edge of the first page. Flux and tack solder in place.

9 Close the book and line up the other part of the box latch with the first so it will close evenly and latch easily. Flux and tack solder in place.

## A Decorative Variation

Adding familiar and decorative items such as lace, ribbon, and even ornate metal embellishments allows you limitless possibilities for personalization. Once you learn the basics of these glass and metal scrapbooks, the sky's the limit as to what you can do.

# Decorative Tin Box

*A new latch makes this once-forgotten tin box more useful than ever before, and the soldered collage charm gives this little box a bigger-than-life attitude.*

## MATERIALS

Decorative paper

Clip art photo

Word stickers

2 pieces of rectangular glass,
    1 x 1¾ inches

Copper foil tape

Lead-free solder

Small tin box, 2½ x 3½ inches

Copper spray paint

2 decorative corners

Decorative box latch

Black permanent ink

Stickers

Clear varnish (optional)

## INSTRUCTIONS

1 Use the paper, clip art photo, and word stickers to create a mini collage. Sandwich your design between the pieces of glass.

2 Wrap the edges with the copper foil tape. Solder all the edges.

3 Spray the tin box with the copper spray paint. Let it dry.

4 Position two decorative corners on the box. Scrape off the paint where the corners will be soldered. Flux the back of the decorative corners. Fill the back side in with solder if needed (see page 33).

5 Place the decorative corners back on top of the box. Flux the box (where the paint has been scraped off). Heat the solder that is on the back of the decorative corner until it melts and flows onto the box. Using pliers to hold it, push the corner into place on the box.

6 Scrape off the paint where the rectangular soldered collage will go. Flux the tin, and solder the collage to the box top.

7 Position the box latch on the front of the box. Line up the pieces so the top and bottom can lock. Scrape the paint away from its position.

8 Flux the back side of each piece of the box latch. Melt solder onto the back of both pieces of the latch and let it cool. Flux the tin, and solder in place.

9 Touch up any copper paint as needed. Sponge the black permanent ink onto the paint and metal pieces covering the box. Wipe away the excess. This will give the box an antique appearance.

10 Place stickers on the top and around the edges.

11 An optional finishing idea: paint clear varnish over the stickers to seal them in place.

# Handmade Frames
# for Special Memories

*Use stickers, charms, beads, and other items to cele-brate the special memory captured in a photograph. It's easy to do, and the stunning results help the memories last a lifetime.*

**INSTRUCTIONS**

1 Make a collage by layering items onto a $3\frac{1}{2}$ x 5-inch piece of decorative background paper. Place your composition between the pieces of glass.

2 Wrap the edges with the copper foil tape.

3 Solder all the edges.

4 Solder the safety pin to a corner of the soldered frame. Leave the opening end of the pin pointing toward the bottom of the frame. Open the pin and slide on your favorite charms, pearls, or even letter beads to spell out your feelings. Close the pin.

5 Solder two large jump rings to the top of the frame. Thread the ribbon through the jump rings, and tie the ends in a knot.

**MATERIALS**

Photo
Stickers of words or phrases
Decorative paper
2 pieces of glass, $3\frac{1}{2}$ x 5 inches
Copper foil tape
Lead-free solder
1 safety pin
Charms, beads, or letter beads
2 large oval jump rings
8 inches of ribbon, $\frac{1}{2}$ inch wide

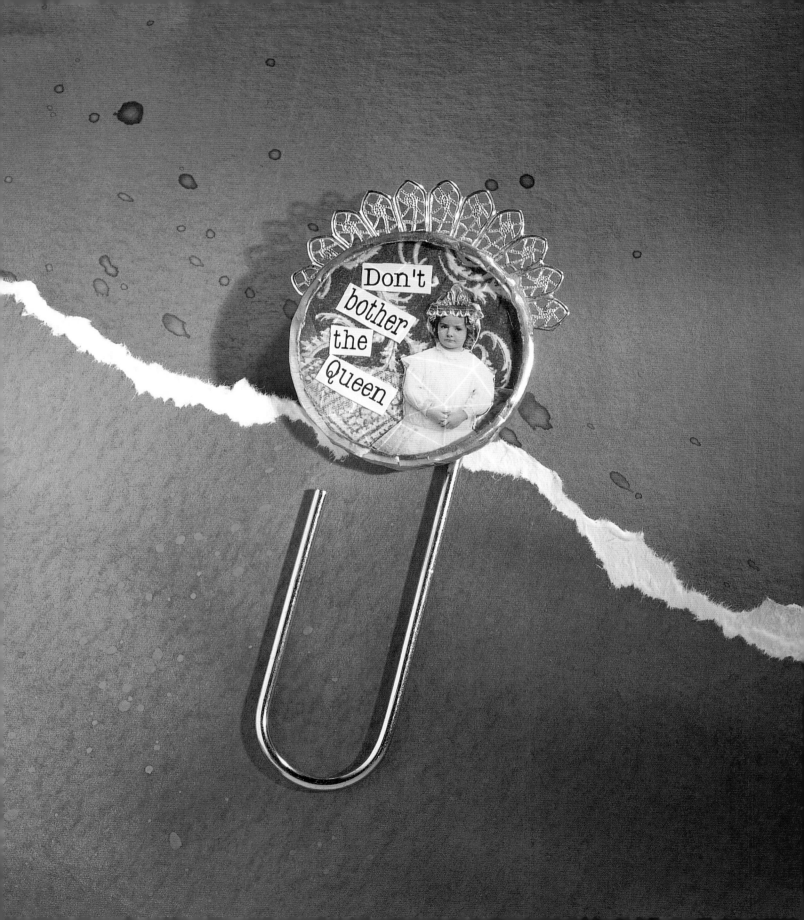

# Fit for a Queen Bookmark

*By using an oversized paper clip and some rather "commanding" clip art, this ornate bookmark makes a big statement.*

## INSTRUCTIONS

1 Trim the paper to fit the glass. Trim or cut out an old photo and adhere it to the background paper. Add any other art work, stickers, or decorations you'd like.

2 Sandwich the composition between the glass and the piece of scrap aluminum.

3 Wrap with edges with the copper foil tape.

4 Solder the edges.

5 Using a clamp, position the decorative filigree on the back of the glass. Apply flux and solder it into place.

6 Use a clamp to position the end of the paper clip against the back of the glass. Apply flux and solder it into place. Be sure to solder the glass on the top end of the paper clip so it will be able to slide down onto a page.

## MATERIALS

Patterned papers
Vintage photo
Round, jewel-beveled glass, ½ inch across
Typed words or phrases
Decorative stickers
Piece of scrap aluminum
Copper foil tape
Lead-free solder
Silver filigree
Giant paper clip

# Vintage Seasonal Celebrations

*Turn old postcards, clip art, and household artifacts into artful celebrations of the seasons.*

**INSTRUCTIONS**

1 Trim the images to fit the glass panels. Position them between the glass and aluminum foil tape.

2 Wrap the edges with the copper foil tape. If you use the wavy foil tape, make sure the wavy side ends up on the front side of the glass.

3 Solder around all the edges.

4 Add seasonal embellishments, charms, ribbons, messages, dangles, or whatever best reflects your feelings about the holidays. Also, be sure to plan ways to hang your ornaments, such as attaching jump rings or wire hangers for ribbons, string, or wire.

5 Apply various styles of finishes as needed. For example, you can sponge acrylic paint on the soldered edges, then sand or scuff the paint to give it an antique look.

**MATERIALS**

Vintage clip art images
Glass panels, 2 x 3 inches each
Aluminum foil tape
Copper foil tape in various forms (wavy, straight, etc.)
Lead-free solder
Decorative ribbons
Various metal or tinned charms
Acrylic paint or other finishing materials

# Classic Bottle Makeover

*Even the most basic soldering and beading techniques can be combined to turn simple glass bottles like these into stylish standouts for your home.*

## INSTRUCTIONS

1 Wrap a strip of the copper foil tape around each bottle.

2 Solder over the tape.

3 Position a decorative wire clip along the soldered strip of one of the bottles. Make sure it's centered. Apply flux and solder it into place. Repeat this for the other two bottles.

4 Cut the legs off six of the jeweled brads. Flux the edges of the brads. Solder them onto the soldered strip next to the wire clips. Be careful not to get these too hot because you could melt the plastic jewel inside.

5 Insert three brads (with the legs still on them) into the top of each cork stopper.

## MATERIALS

3 bottles with cork stoppers
Copper foil tape
Lead-free solder
Large diamond-shaped
　paper clip
2 large spiral paper clips
9 jeweled brads of various
　colors

There never has been,
nor will there ever be,
anything quite so special
as the love between
a mother and her sons.

S
O
N
S

# Dressed-Up Photo Album

*A simple photo album can become as delightful and distinct on the outside as the memories it keeps on the inside. Redefine the whole experience by creating a unique framed photo and page tabs as a decorative introduction to the story.*

## INSTRUCTIONS

1 Print a favorite quote or phrase on some attractive paper. Mat the photo with paper that contrasts the paper bearing the quote or phrase. Add the matted photo to the printed piece of paper. Sandwich this composition between the glass and the aluminum foil tape.

2 Wrap the edges with the copper foil tape. Solder around all the edges.

3 Solder the decorative spiral clips to the top and bottom edges.

4 Place the epoxy magnifying sticker over a specific word to highlight it.

5 Thread the ribbon through one spiral clip, behind the glass, and up through the other clip. Tie the ends of the ribbon around the front cover of the book.

6 Place the letter stickers on paper backgrounds that match the paper used in step 1. Trim the letters to fit under the glass pieces. Sandwich the paper between the pieces of glass and the aluminum foil tape. Wrap the edges with the copper foil tape. Solder the edges.

7 Position a letter charm on the outer edge of a badge clip. Flux the clip, and solder the letter charm to the clip. Repeat this process until you have enough to spell a favorite word.

8 Attach the clips to pages in the album to spell a word along the edge.

### MATERIALS

Printed quote or favorite phrase
Eye-catching paper
Photo
Contrasting paper for matting the photo
Glass rectangle, 2 x 3 inches
Aluminum foil tape
Copper foil tape
Lead-free solder
2 large decorative wire clips
Small, clear epoxy magnifying sticker
16 inches of ribbon, $\frac{1}{2}$ inch wide
Small photo album
Letter stickers
Paper that coordinates with the letter clippings
4 pieces of glass, $\frac{7}{8}$ x $\frac{3}{4}$ inch
4 name badge clips

# Embellished Candle Holders and Votives

*Whether you need candles as a functional accessory in a room, or just a whimsical decorative pick-me-up, these embellished candle holders will do either job in spades.*

## Elegant Candle Stems

### INSTRUCTIONS

1 Wrap a strip of the copper foil tape around the bottom edge of each candle holder cup.

2 Solder over the tape. Remember, when soldering on a round surface, turn the piece as you're soldering to help the solder flow evenly.

3 Use pliers to curve the scroll clips to lie flush against the edge of the glass.

4 Use a clamp or pliers to hold the wire clip against the soldered strip. Tack solder it in place. Space the clips evenly around the bottom edge. Make sure the loops of the wire clips extend past the bottom edge of the glass.

5 Thread two round crystal beads onto each of the head pins, and make a loop at the ends. Trim the ends of the wires. Attach these to every other spiral of the scrolled decorative clips.

6 Thread the eye pins through the teardrop beads. Bend the end of the wire up and in (to form a triangle). Clip the end of the wire where it meets the loop on the pin. Attach the dangles to the spirals not filled in step 5.

### MATERIALS

Copper foil tape
Purchased glass candle holders
Lead-free solder
10 scrolled wire clips
20 faceted, clear round beads, 6 mm
10 head pins
10 faceted, clear teardrop beads, 10 mm
10 eye pins

# Glass Votive Trio

**INSTRUCTIONS**

1 Wrap a strip of copper foil tape around each votive. Solder over the tape.

2 Solder jump rings onto the wavy part of the soldered area, skipping every other scallop for spacing.

3 Make dangles for the votives by placing two beads of the same color on the head pins. Make loops at the ends of each. Trim the excess wire from each dangle. Keep doing this until you have created enough bead dangles for each votive.

4 Attach the dangles to the jump rings on the votives, alternating bead colors as you go. Be sure to leave one spot for the soldered charm on each votive.

5 Cut the pictures to fit the glass, then sandwich the pictures and glass together.

6 Wrap with the edges with the regular copper foil tape (the type with the straight edge).

7 Solder the edges of the three charms.

8 Solder a jump ring to the top edge of each charm. Make sure the jump rings are centered.

9 Thread two beads of different colors onto each of the three eye pins and make loops at the ends of each. Attach the glass charms to the jump rings on the votive with the beaded eye pins.

**MATERIALS**

Wavy copper foil tape

3 glass votives

Lead-free solder

36 small jump rings

30 metal daisy beads

22 green beads, 2 mm

22 pink beads, 2 mm

22 yellow beads, 2 mm

30 head pins

3 floral pictures in colors that match glass and beads

6 pieces of glass, 1 x ¾ inch

Regular copper foil tape

3 eye pins

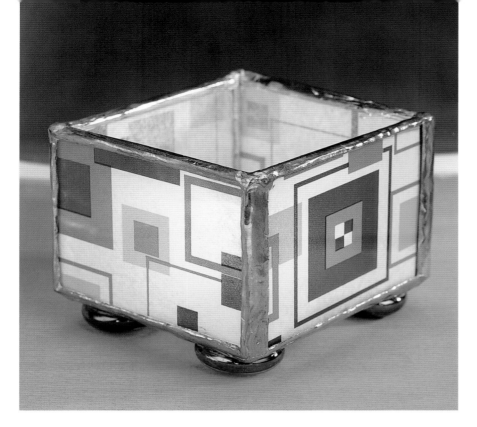

*Figure 1*

# Glass Box and Candle Holder

## INSTRUCTIONS

1 Cut the tissue paper or photos to fit between four sets of glass panels. Fit the paper and glass together.

2 Wrap each panel's edge with the copper foil tape.

3 Solder the edges of all the panels.

4 Line up two sides of the box, placing one panel inside the edge of the other (see figure 1). Tack solder it in place.

5 Line up another side of the box, making sure the glass sides are positioned on the inside edge of the box. Tack solder into place.

6 Add the last panel, making sure the position of the glass is the same as the glass wall opposite to it.

7 Wrap the bottom piece of glass with the copper foil tape, and solder all the edges.

8 Position the bottom piece, and solder around all the edges.

9 Go back over all seams and add more solder to fill in any gaps.

10 Glue four flat back marbles to the bottom of the box.

## MATERIALS

Decorative tissue paper or photos
8 glass panels, 3½ x 2½ inches
Copper foil tape
Lead-free solder
Glass panel for the bottom,
    3¼ x 3½ inches
Glass glue
4 flat back glass marbles

# Picture Perfect Pixie Collages

*These playful pieces—which can be used as ornaments, gift tags, or tiny works of art—are full of attitude. Maybe that's why they're my favorite projects to make. Each collage is built on four pieces of glass. When the layers are stacked and soldered together, a complete picture is made.*

**MATERIALS**

Pixie clip art
4 pieces of glass, 2 x 3 inches
Decorative paper
Word clip art or stickers
Copper foil tape
Lead-free solder
Various embellishments, such as ribbon, wire, jump rings, head pins, eye pins, filigrees, beads, etc. (as needed)

*A small library of pixie clip art is available on page 141 to help you get started.*

HELPFUL TIP: Before gluing anything into place, position the elements on each new layer of glass as you build the piece. Once you're certain everything lines up, glue the pieces into place.

## Standing Pixies

**INSTRUCTIONS**

1  Cut out a Standing Pixie photo (showing a complete, standing figure) and any other images (wings, crowns, words, flowers, etc.) you want to include.

2  Alter the pixie as necessary. Example: if your pixie needs a crown or other head wear, trim away some of the hair so the crown appears to "fit" her head.

3  Choose your background paper for the first layer of glass (what will end up as the bottom piece when everything is assembled). Glue the paper to the glass and trim any excess from the edges.

4 On the second layer of glass, line up things such as wings and the pixie's legs, then glue them into place. Add the words and phrases you've chosen for this pixie onto this layer of glass.

5 Place the third layer of glass on top of the second. Line up the pixie's body over the wings and legs. Glue the torso into place.

6 Assemble your pixie. Stack the first three layers together, making sure everything lines up correctly, then add the fourth piece of glass.

7 Clamp all the pieces together firmly, but not so hard as to crack the glass.

8 Wrap the edges with the ½ inch copper foil tape.

9 Solder all the edges.

NOTE: I love using vintage photos. There's a quality about them that just begs to be turned into something lighthearted and fun. Perhaps you'll choose something different. Pet photos, maybe?

# Portrait Pixies

NOTE: Another option for finishing these unique pieces is to wrap the piece in copper foil tape and not solder them. There's an example of this above entitled "Scrapbook Pixie."

**INSTRUCTIONS**

1 Cut out a Portrait Pixie photo (head and shoulders only) and any other images you want to include.

2 Alter the pixie as necessary to fit crowns or other head wear.

3 Choose your background paper for the first layer of glass. Glue the paper to the glass and trim any excess from the edges.

4 On the second layer of glass, place the pixie photo on the glass to make sure it and its crown fit properly. Glue the pieces into place.

5 Place the third layer of glass on top of the second. If you wish to add a piece of paper across the bottom or along the side as a design element, do it on this layer. Helpful hint: avoid adding thick pieces of cloth, such as woven lace. When you press it all together, thick objects will cause the glass to crack. Add the words and phrases you've chosen for this pixie onto this layer of glass.

6 Assemble your pixie. Stack the first three layers together, making sure everything lines up correctly, then add the fourth piece of glass to make the top.

7 Clamp all the pieces together firmly, but not so hard that you crack the glass.

8 Wrap the edges with the ½ inch copper foil tape.

9 Solder all the edges.

NOTE: Pixies are so versatile, the sky's the limit when it comes to decorating them. Solder jump rings to the bottom edge for beaded dangles, attach filigrees, decorative corners, decorative metal objects, or just about any object you might find.

# Signature Gift and Display Ideas

Now that you're making soldered jewelry and other unique things for the home, you'll no doubt want to share your work with you're your friends and family. Who knows, you may even want to try your hand at selling pieces online or at gift markets. In either event, here are some ideas for giving your pieces the ideal finishing touch, and then presenting your work in a unique and professional manner.

Since you're essentially designing your own logo and signature packaging, there are no right or wrong answers. Just let your personality and sense of style shine through.

## Custom Signature Metal Tags

Make custom tags for your pieces by flattening a small amount of solder using a hammer and small anvil or steel block. When the solder is thin enough, you'll be able to stamp your initials or a specific design into the metal. The wonderful thing about working with solder is how easily it can be shaped. Any number of utensils can do the trick, including wire cutters, scissors, and files. Experiment and find ways that best suits your design ideas. Just remember, you want to find a way of creating the design consistently.

## Decorative Boxes and Wraps

Altering purchased jewelry boxes is an easy way to create a distinct look for your designs. Simply wrap the boxes with printed cardstock, then add ribbon and a unique "logo" tag. People will know they're getting a rare one-of-a-kind gift.

## Plastic Envelope Displays

Print your logo and special design on cardstock and use it to display your work. Trim the cardstock to fit into plastic envelopes. Position the jewelry where you want it, then cut slits in the paper with scissors or a craft knife. Slide the pieces into the slits, then fit the card into the sleeves.

## Picture Frame Displays

If you decide to dive into selling your soldered art at gift markets or craft fairs, here's a great idea for displaying your work in a way that's fun and professional. Cut some foam core to fit inside a picture frame. Cover the foam core with fabric, then mount the piece onto the back of the frame (I've found that duct tape does the job nicely). All you have to do next is use T-pins to mount your pieces directly onto the foam, stand or hang the frame, and wait for the sales to roll in.

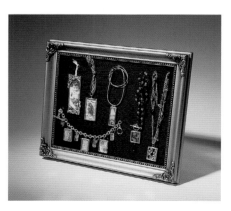

Scrapbook Pixie    Pouty Pixie
She always had to have her way   create
it was enough for her to just be pretty
Prima Pixie   Compose    capture

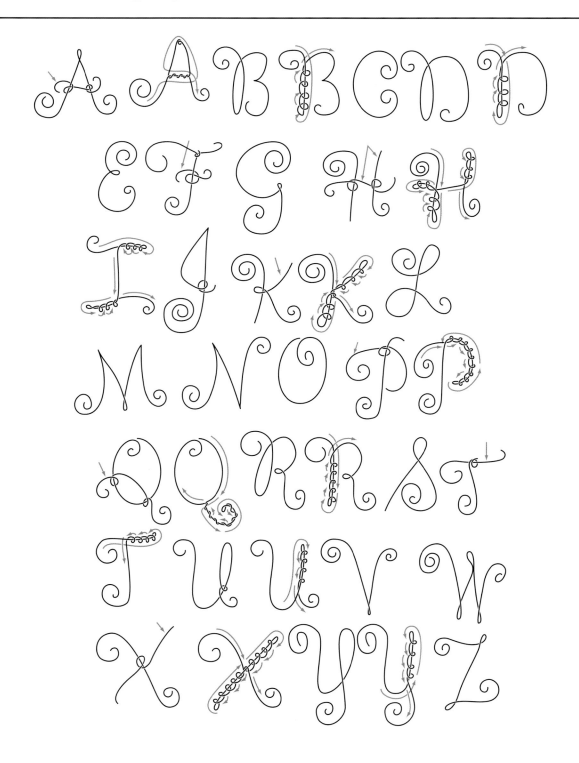